AF249321

Go to the Games with

Go to the Games with

KERN TIPS *and the* GOLDEN AGE *of* SWC *radio*

ALAN BURTON

Anarene Books

COPYRIGHT©2019 BY ALAN BURTON
All rights reserved.

ISBN: 978-0-578-51644-8

Written permission must be secured from the publisher or the author to use or reproduce any part of this book, except for brief quotations in critical reviews or articles.

Cover design and Page layout by Goofidity Designs
Cover Photo: Humble announcer Kern Tips (courtesy of Texas Sports Hall of Fame)

PHOTO CREDITS:

Baker University Athletics; ExxonMobil Corporation; New Mexico Sports Hall of Fame; akdart.com; Faingold Photography; Juan M. Garcia; John Morris, Baylor University Athletics; Kansas Association of Broadcasters; News/Talk95.1 & 790 KFYO, Lubbock, Texas; Dan Lovett; Texas Association of Broadcasters; Ronnie Perry; Wayne Keeling; Lee Klancher; Susan Munguia; Pennsylvania Sports Hall of Fame; J. R. Phillips; Houston Astros Baseball Club; Los Angeles Dodgers Baseball Club; LSU Athletics; TCU Athletics; Connie Alexander Play-by-Play Sports Broadcasting collection, Center for Southwest Research & Special Collections, University of New Mexico; Hans J. Wollstein, Texas Sports Hall of Fame.

PRINTED IN THE UNITED STATES OF AMERICA

TO MY DAD,
who took me to football games at an early age.

And to all those dedicated broadcasters
who took me to the games with

Humble.

CONTENTS

ACKNOWLEDGMENTS

The author wishes to thank a number of individuals for their assistance during the process of researching and writing *Go to the Games with Humble*, including Jay Black and Paige Davis of the Texas Sports Hall of Fame, Beth Bobbitt of the Texas Association of Broadcasters, Michael Bonnettee and Jason Feirman with LSU Athletics, Roland Brown, Thomas "Joe Fan" Ciaburri of El Paso, Mark Cohen with TCU Athletics, Kent Cornish of the Kansas Association of Broadcasters, A. K. Dart, Dr. John Mark Dempsey, Bill Douglass and Brad Douglass of Douglass Distributing in Sherman (Texas), Glenn Dromgoole, Dr. Ryan Ellett, Kathy Elliott, David Faingold of Faingold Photography, and Kyle Pattrick with Baker University.

Also, Steve Fallon, Mike Fallon, Juan M. Garcia, Leslie Barker Garcia, Mitchell Glieber, Dana Hall of the Seguin (Texas) Chamber of Commerce, Tinyah Hawkins, Josh Holstead of the Texas Radio Hall of Fame, Joe Jareck and Mark Langill of the Los Angeles Dodgers, Jacob Pomrenke of the Society for American Baseball Research, Tomas Jaehn, Portia Vescio, and Samuel Sisneros of the Center for Southwest Research & Special Collections, University of New Mexico Libraries, Tom Hedrick, Wayne Keeling, Lee Klancher, Jeff Limberg, Dan Lovett, Charlotte Manzone of BBDO NY, Susan Mungia, John Morris with Baylor Athletics, Ronnie Perry, J. R. Phillips, Gene Pino with the New Mexico Sports Hall of Fame, Dave Ritting, Tumbleweed Smith, Mike Towle, Hans J. Wollstein, Rob Snyder of KFYO in Lubbock, and Steve Grande and Dominic Holden of the Houston Astros.

And a special thanks to ExxonMobil Corporation.

Football broadcasters and telecasters are lucky guys; and when they work in the Southwest Conference, they are thriced-blessed with fine coaches, outstanding officiating and terrific football players. Truly, ours is a privileged profession.

—Kern Tips, 1957

(The Power and the Glory—The Story of Southwest Conference Football)

INTRODUCTION

My formal introduction to big-time college football took place on Saturday, October 17, 1964, in the Cotton Bowl.

The cool, crisp autumn evening featured the Rice Owls (1-2) versus the hometown Southern Methodist University Mustangs (1-2) in a Southwest Conference game. It mattered little that only 20,000 spectators ventured into the cavernous stadium (75,504 capacity) for the eight o'clock kickoff. Although the game itself was hardly memorable (Rice won, 7-6), it was an unforgettable experience for a wide-eyed seven-year-old. Accompanied by my parents and older brother and armed with a $4 general admission ticket, I settled into my designated seat in Section 123, Row 11.

Setting foot in the historic Cotton Bowl, situated on the Texas State Fair grounds and just a few miles from the downtown Dallas site where President John F. Kennedy was assassinated a year earlier, was indeed memorable.

Being a rabid Texas Longhorns fan at the time, I was thrilled to be able to purchase an orange and white UT pennant at the game, which I still have—fifty-five years later. Although the Rice-SMU game was anything but a classic, headlines were being made two hundred miles to the south in Austin that same evening, when the Arkansas Razorbacks upset the top-ranked and defending national champion Longhorns, 14-13.

One thing the two games had in common was that fans across the state could follow all the play-by-play action on the radio, thanks to the Humble Oil and Refining

This is the cover of the game program from the 1964 Rice-SMU contest played in the Cotton Bowl.

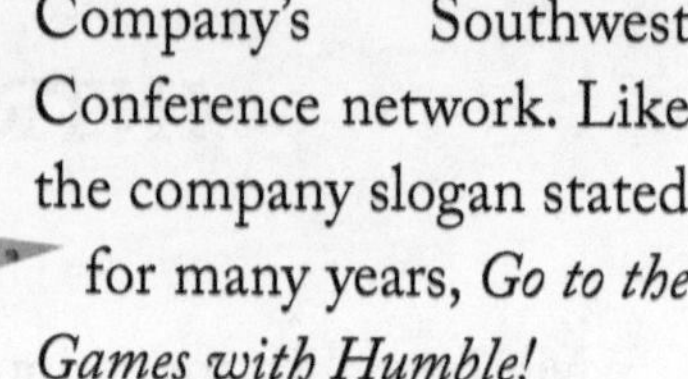

The author's University of Texas pennant, purchased at the Rice-SMU game in 1964.

Company's Southwest Conference network. Like the company slogan stated for many years, *Go to the Games with Humble!*

Fast forward to Thanksgiving, 1968.

Now a wide-eyed eleven-year-old, I piled into our tank with my family. It happened to be a brand-new, maroon and white '68 Buick LeSabre with a sticker price of $3,800, and with it we made the 324-mile drive west from Sherman to Lubbock for Thanksgiving dinner with relatives.

The six-hour drive (it seemed liked sixteen as we encountered the remnants of a light snowfall) along Highway 82 took us through such landmark destinations as Wichita Falls, Seymour (still my personal favorite), Benjamin, Guthrie, Dickens, Crosbyton, and Ralls, until we finally arrived in Lubbock. On the way, thanks to Humble and the car radio, we managed to monitor—with a few transmission interruptions, courtesy of the picturesque Caprock— the Texas A&M-Texas game from Austin, with Connie Alexander behind the microphone.

Arriving in Lubbock, we then ventured a few miles southwest to the rural cotton-farming community of Ropesville, where we

For many years, this building served as a cafe for workers and customers of Buster's Gin in Ropesville, Texas. This photo was taken in 2019. (courtesy of Wayne Keeling)

joined my cousins for a delicious complimentary Thanksgiving meal at Buster's Gin Cafe. The cafe, a cinder-block building, could have been a perfect set piece for *The Last Picture Show*.

While we knew none of the diners (cotton gin employees and customers) other than our relatives, they couldn't have been more hospitable. My dad, being the stand-up guy he was and is, offered to pay for our turkey and dressing since we didn't qualify as gin employees or cotton farmers. But the quiet, mysterious gin owner with a fedora hat and sly grin named Buster said that wouldn't be necessary.

Afterward, we returned to our relatives' farmhouse to listen to the conclusion of the

The counter and chairs from the cafe at Buster's Gin now reside in Dan Taylor's shop and museum in Ropesville, Texas. Taylor is a former owner of the gin. (courtesy of Lee Klancher)

Longhorns' wishbone-led 35-14 victory, with James Street at quarterback.

As a footnote, C. O. "Buster" McNabb passed away in 1990; however, Buster's Gin, which opened in 1947, is still in business today. The building that housed the cafe is also still standing, but is now used for storage.

Long before the advent of ESPN, the explosion of cable TV sports, and, eventually, the launch of the Longhorn Network, college football fans tuned in their radios to follow the SWC teams. Humble, with its broadcast origins dating back to 1934, offered unbiased play-by-play action of all conference teams through the vast number—at least in later years—of radio stations on its statewide network.

Whether you were outside working in the yard, riding in the car, visiting Aunt Mabel, hunting, fishing, tossing a football around, or just sitting on the porch, the games were just a fingertip away. For that we could thank the technology of the radio, later the car radio (first offered commercially in the 1930s, but not common until the 1950s), and still later, the transistor radio (introduced by Texas Instruments in 1954).

Humble/Enco/Exxon (H/E/E) sponsored SWC football radio broadcasts for forty-four consecutive years, from 1934 to 1977. This was noteworthy because, during most of that time, few games were televised; viewers were limited to a minimal number of national and regional games of the week.

Due to various changes in the company, branding and advertising evolved over the years. From 1934-1960, fans were urged to "Go to the Games with Humble;" from 1961-72, it was "Go to the Games with Enco;" and from 1973-77, the branding had changed from Enco to Exxon. But it remained the same reliable network through all those years and changes.

In today's saturated world of college games on television and school-operated radio networks, the old days of radio, in many ways, seem better. Much was left to the listener's imagination, and there's nothing wrong with that.

For instance, H/E/E play-by-play announcer Connie Alexander's description of the pageantry of Memorial Stadium in Austin made it sound like the Roman Colosseum (it wasn't just a loud crowd, it was a "Vesuvius of Voices," according to Connie). A few years later, when I saw the stadium in person for the first time, I was mildly disappointed.

The king of the Humble-Enco microphone from 1935 until his death in the summer of 1967 was golden-throated Kern Tips, a former sportswriter, radio and advertising executive from Houston. His unique, cliché-filled play-by-play mesmerized and entertained listeners. He was known as "the Voice of Texas Football" and "the Voice of the Southwest Conference"—take your pick.

Tips's legacy lives on today in Texas literature and culture. Dan Jenkins's novel *Fast Copy*, which depicts newspaper life in the late 1930s, features protagonist Betsy Throckmorton Winton, a character recognized for her radio impersonation of Tips. Likewise, in his book *Texas Sportswriters—the Wild and Wacky Years*, Bob St. John recalls that in the early 1970s, fellow *Dallas Morning News* sportswriters John Anders and Mike Jones would entertain the newsroom with imitations of Tips and color announcer Alec Chesser.

Tom Pilkington, in his collection of essays titled *State of Mind: Texas Literature and Culture*, begins a chapter on football by recalling growing up in the fifties and listening to Tips's descriptive voice on the radio.

Even years after his death, Tips is fondly remembered in a poem that is found elsewhere in this book.

(Full disclosure: for the most part, Tips's play-by-play stint predated my network listening days, so I don't remember him well. My two favorite play-by-play guys were the aforementioned Connie Alexander and Jack Dale, with my top sidekicks being Stan McKenzie and Dave Smith.)

Perhaps another well-known Dallas sportswriter-author, Gary Cartwright, put it best in an ode to the SWC in an October 30, 1995, *Sports Illustrated* article about the breakup of the league:

It would be hard to exaggerate the excitement that the first kiss of autumn generated at all levels of society. As early as 1934, the air was literally filled with Southwest Conference football, thanks to the Humble Radio Network, the nation's first broadcast network. You couldn't visit a drugstore or barbershop or even walk along a sidewalk without hearing the roar of the crowd and the boom of the marching bands at Kyle Field or the Cotton Bowl—or the voice of Humble's master of word pictures, Kern Tips. . . . You didn't have to be college-educated to have a favorite team. Service stations operated by Humble Oil & Refining Company (now

Exxon), which also owned the radio network, gave out pennant-shaped window decals, each with the colors and name of a conference school. Bank presidents with degrees from SMU and pipe fitters who hadn't finished third grade displayed their choice on the rear window of their cars. Millions of Texans from Beaumont to Laredo to Amarillo never saw a game but lived and died from Saturday to Saturday with the Frogs, the Mustangs, the Bears, the Longhorns, the Aggies, the Owls, the Hogs, and, later, the Red Raiders and the Cougars.

Many boys grew up in Texas hearing about such heroes as Sammy Baugh, Doak Walker, Bobby Layne, Kyle Rote, John David Crow, Tommy Nobis, Earl Campbell, and countless others described in larger-than-life words by the reliable H/E/E announcing crews. Adding to the excitement was the collateral of collectibles available at H/E/E service stations, including schedules, decals, bumper stickers, commemorative coins, drinking glasses, pennants, and the like. And in the early days, *The Humble Football News*, a tabloid with feature articles by Texas sportswriters, was distributed free each Thursday at Humble stations. It was quite a marketing effort, especially for the time.

The Humble Football News was distributed weekly during football season at the company's service stations throughout Texas. (courtesy of Ronnie Perry)

The H/E/E association with SWC football ended more than 40 years ago (after the 1977 season), 19 years before the demise of the conference itself. (To put that into perspective, another oil company—Shell— sponsored the highly popular *Shell's Wonderful World of Golf* on TV for "only" 10 years (1961-70), although the series was reborn in 1994.)

So why, after all these years, should we care about these

To promote the SWC radio broadcasts, Humble-Enco-Exxon service stations offered customers free collectibles, such as this set of coins. (courtesy of Ronnie Perry)

voices of the past?

One reason is because the stories of these dedicated announcers, few of whom are still living, have never been fully told. (Through research, at least eighty-five gentlemen have been identified as having worked one or more games during the 44-year reign of the H/E/E network.) Times were simpler during their pre-internet and instant information era. These politely-spoken gentlemen at the microphone, most of whom were faceless to us, nevertheless brightened up our Saturdays with their professional, engaging, and entertaining broadcasts.

Theirs was a warm, genuine love and appreciation for the game, and that came through loud and clear on the radio. Adding to the mystique of the broadcasts was that, at least in the early days, many of the announcers had intriguing names, such as Fort Pearson, Ves Box, Coit Butler, Tee Casper, Conrad Brady, Guy Savage, Bob Tongo, Cy Leland, Byrum Saam, Fritz Kuler, Fred Nahas, and Harfield Weeden.

Then there were the more familiar names, or famous-to-be names, including Kern Tips, Gordon McLendon, Jerry Doggett, Frank Glieber, Frank Fallon, Connie Alexander, Gene Elston, Eddie Barker, and Dan Lovett, all of whom, at one time or another, sat behind the H/E/E microphone. More than a half-dozen other announcers went on to achieve notoriety in the television and motion picture industry (but more on that later).

Go to the Games with Humble is not only a history of SWC football on the radio, but also a celebration and appreciation of all the talented, but unseen play-by-play and color announcers who faithfully provided listeners a weekly link to their favorite teams.

Now, let's return to those thrilling radio days of yesteryear.

Happy Reading!

HUMBLE BEGINNINGS

The Humble Oil Company was chartered in Texas in 1911; it was reorganized in 1917 and incorporated as the Humble Oil and Refining Company.

The original company involved a collaboration of Ross S. Sterling and Walter William Fondren, with Robert L. Blaffer, William Stamps Farish, and others. Ross Sterling would later serve as the thirty-first governor of Texas, from 1931-33.

In February of 1919, Humble sold 50 percent of its stock to Standard Oil Company of New Jersey. This initiated Humble's long-term connection with the company that eventually absorbed it as Exxon Company. U.S.A. Standard Oil was identified as the particular target of antitrust enforcers in Texas in the early decades of the twentieth century, which is why the corporation found it much easier to do business in the state through Humble, its partially owned but autonomously directed affiliate.

Humble became the largest domestic producer of crude oil during World War II, and it continued in that position into the 1950s. By the end of 1949, the Humble Pipe Line Company, a subsidiary, had amassed 3,233 miles of gathering lines and 5,776 miles of trunk lines. These facilities served important producing areas in Texas and southeastern New Mexico, and the Humble Pipe Line Company was the largest transporter of crude oil in the United States.

In the postwar period, the company built a pipeline from Baytown to the Dallas-Fort Worth area. In June of 1950, it completed an eighteen-inch direct line from West Texas to the Gulf Coast.

Humble refineries during World War II produced high-octane aviation gasoline, toluene for explosives, Butyl rubber, and butadiene for synthetic rubber. In the 1940s, Humble products were retailed only in Texas.

In the 1950s, Standard Oil of New Jersey began to reconsider its relationship with Humble Oil. In spite of the fact that Standard owned almost 88 percent of Humble's stock in 1954, Humble continued to maintain its autonomy for the rest of the decade. In 1958, Standard increased its holdings to some 98 percent of Humble's stock, and the following year, Humble and Standard Oil of New Jersey consolidated domestic operations.

About a year later, in September of 1959, Humble received a new charter from the state of Delaware. By the end of the year, Esso Standard and the Carter Oil Company, other affiliates of Standard of New Jersey, were incorporated into Humble, and in 1960, they were joined by other affiliates, including Enjay Chemical, Pate Oil, Globe Fuel Products, and Oklahoma Oil.

The restructuring allowed the new Humble company to reduce duplication and costs, and allowed for more effective coordination of all of its domestic activities. The Humble workforce dropped by a quarter in the first five years after the merger, while its profits doubled.

Humble began to increase its retailing outlets in the 1950s and 1960s. By 1961, it was reaching markets in twenty-one states. By 1951, Humble had become the leading marketer of gasoline in Texas, and its share of the state market continued to increase through the decade, furthered by its creative marketing techniques.

Humble was the first gasoline company to issue plastic gasoline credit cards in Texas. In 1961, the company began to sell its gasoline as Enco gas in nineteen states, but retained the old brand name of Humble in Texas and Ohio. Esso, the brand name of Standard of New Jersey, continued to be used on the East Coast. In 1964, Humble launched the popular "Put a Tiger in Your Tank" advertising campaign. In earlier years, "Happy Motoring!" was a well-known tag line used by Humble.

In the 1960s and early 1970s, management of both Humble and Standard Oil of New Jersey had become increasingly concerned about the lack of a unified public corporate identity. At the same time, the other Standard Oil companies were raising objections to the use of the word Esso, derived from the first letters of the words *Standard Oil*, as the brand name for Humble and Standard of New Jersey gasoline products.

In early 1972, Humble and Standard of New Jersey announced that their gasoline products were to be marketed as Exxon, that Standard of New Jersey was changing its name to Exxon Corporation, and that, as of January 1, 1973, Humble was changing its name to Exxon Company, U.S.A.

In 1990, Exxon Corporation moved its corporate headquarters from New York City to Irving, Texas.

In December of 1998, Exxon Corporation and Mobil Corporation announced their intent to merge because the companies had enjoyed a strategic business relationship for several years in a number of international ventures; the merger was finalized on November 30, 1999.

The merger proved to be a great success. With a combined workforce, expanded knowledge, and increased efficiencies, ExxonMobil Corporation has proven itself a global energy leader, known for its focus on safety and environmental protection, project execution, capital efficiency, and technological innovation.

———— ———— ———— ———— ————

In 1912, University of Minnesota Professor F. W. Springer and an instructor named H. M. Turner started an experimental radio station with the call numbers 9X1-WLB. As part of this project, the two men broadcast accounts of University of Minnesota home football games to a small audience. According to Ronald A. Smith, writing in *Play-by-Play: Radio, Television, and Big-Time College Sport*, this was believed to be the first use of wireless telegraphy to broadcast a college sporting event.

Eight years later, in College Station, Texas, three cadets—B. Lewis Nelson, Harry M. Saunders, and W. A. "Doc" Tolson—rigged up a crude telegraph machine and broadcast Texas A&M's 7-0 victory over the University of Texas back to Austin. This was two years before KDKA (Pittsburgh) broadcast the first prize fight and first major league baseball game, and three years before WEAF (New York) originated voice broadcasts from football games.

According to *Play-by-Play*, the July 1921 broadcast of the Jack Dempsey-Georges Carpentier heavyweight championship fight on WJY (Newark, New Jersey) was one of the key events in the development of radio broadcasting. The broadcast event also produced the first major sportscaster—Major Andrew J. White. White was also publisher of the *RCA Journal* and acting president of the National Amateur Wireless Association. Via transmitter, his voice was carried to a railroad terminal two miles from the fight. From there, J. O. Smith, an associate of White, repeated the description to the listening audience.

KDKA offered the first live radio broadcast of a college football game on October 8, 1921, with the West Virginia-Pittsburgh contest. Harold Arlin handled play-by-play duties.

The first actual radio broadcast of a football game in Texas took place on November 26, 1925, from College Station. General Ike Ashburn, a former Texas A&M commandant, handled the play-by-play of the Aggies' 28-0 victory over Texas.

But over the next few years, as the interest in the new technology and college football grew, so did some concerns. Many schools believed that the broadcasting of games was hurting game attendance and thus revenue. This, combined with the country's economic depression, was having a negative impact on gate receipts. In fact, radio broadcasts were banned during the 1932 season by the Eastern Intercollegiate Association (Ivy League schools plus Army, Navy, Penn State, and Syracuse), the Southern Conference, and the Southwest Conference.

(Ironically, some of the same concerns and issues would emerge circa 1950 with the beginning of college football telecasts. Those disagreements and legal battles over TV rights would continue for many years as the NCAA tried to control TV rights.)

But by the mid-1930s, schools realized that, in addition to positive exposure, there was money to be made through commercial radio broadcasting rights. Plus, by then, the general public was becoming used to the idea of listening to games on the radio; taking that away would have been a public relations issue for the schools.

As a result, schools/conferences began making deals with such networks and sponsors as NBC, Don Lee-Columbia Broadcasting System, Hearst Radio Service, Ohio Oil Company, Atlantic Refining Company, and others. A couple of schools—Michigan and Iowa— signed agreements with slightly different sponsors, Kellogg's Corn Flakes and the Maytag Washing Machine Company.

By 1935, 37 of 72 major institutions had their games broadcast, and 24 of those 37 had sold their rights.

In Texas, during the 1934 season, the Humble Oil and Refining Company broadcast three Rice University games over a three-station network—KPRC in Houston, WOAI in San Antonio, and WFAA in Dallas.

A sold-out showdown at Rice Stadium (18,000 capacity) on October 27, 1934, between Texas and Rice had fans clamoring for a radio broadcast. Humble and Duncan Coffee sponsored the broadcast, in which the play-by-play was forgettably handled by *Houston Post* sports editor Lloyd Gregory.

Gregory recalled the experience in his 1968 autobiography, *Looking 'em Over:*

"We broadcast from an open press box. I knew the Rice players well enough, and did not have a Rice spotter. We did enlist a Texas student who said he knew the Texas players.

"Imagine my consternation when the Texas players came on the field wearing numerals about two inches high.

"Rice kicked off to Texas, and I glanced at my so-called Texas spotter to identify the player running back the kick. *He shook his head!*

"Brother, I may as well confess that I 'choked,' and my slow, colorless report on the game angered thousands of listeners. You should have seen some of the telegrams received between halves.

"Fortunately, I sort of got the hang, and did a much better job in the second half. Many listeners insist to this good day that a different guy broadcast the second half."

The second game broadcast was the Rice-Arkansas contest, originating from Fayetteville, Arkansas, on November 10, 1934.

It, too, was not without problems.

It seems that as the game began, telegraphers in the press box began to send their game reports to newspapers. Unfortunately, the clattering noise of the telegraph keys and electrical interference from the telegraphic instruments caused a garbling noise on the broadcast lines. Complaints then flooded the Humble switchboards. After the broadcast crew was notified of the problem, they went off the air for 15 minutes, packed up all their equipment, and moved across the field to the stands, where they resumed broadcasting.

In 1935, the Magnolia Petroleum Company broadcast a few SWC football games, while Humble sponsored six broadcasts that same fall.

"(But) the next year (1936) they (Magnolia) got ready to do it, the conference wanted to put the thing up for bids," noted Morrell Ratcliffe, an advertising representative for Magnolia in Richard Schroeder's *Texas Signs On: The Early Days of Radio and Television.* "The Humble Oil and Refining Company bid five thousand per school, and Magnolia did not think that it was worth it."

Instead, Magnolia began broadcasting Texas high school football and basketball games.

After a shaky start in 1934, Humble struck oil when, on September 21, 1935, a thirty-one-year-old Houston radio general manager/former sports editor was picked to do the play-by-play of the Rice-St. Mary's game.

His name?

Kern Tips.

THE VOICE OF THE SOUTHWEST CONFERENCE

The advent of radio and college football broadcasts created an urgent need for competent sports announcers. In most cases, sportswriters and radio station announcers were the most logical choices to man the microphones.

But, like with Lloyd Gregory, the results were not always satisfactory. Grantland Rice, one of the most famous sportswriters in history, tried his hand announcing major league baseball. He admittedly was never comfortable in that role, and quickly resumed writing full-time.

And in 1932, a little-known, twenty-one-year-old called Iowa Hawkeye football games before enjoying a successful career in motion pictures and politics. His name: Ronald Reagan.

Two individuals who did emerge as stellar broadcasters early on were Graham McNamee and Ted Husing.

McNamee was a Minneapolis native who moved to New York City at age nineteen to study music and voice. He joined WEAF in New York and burst onto the announcing scene in 1923 doing boxing and baseball. He quickly gained a following, and, by 1925, he and his "pointer" (spotter) Phil Carlin were working intersectional college football games.

Sportswriter Heywood Broun once noted that McNamee was "able to take a new medium of expression and through it transmit himself—to give out vividly a sense of movement and of feeling."

By the 1930s, McNamee was considered by many as the best sports broadcaster in the nation, with Ted Husing also in the conversation.

Husing signed on as a radio announcer at New York's WJZ in 1924. He called the Pennsylvania-Cornell football game in 1925, Boston Braves baseball for a short time, and then Columbia University football games in 1927.

By 1927, Husing had signed with the Columbia Phonograph Broadcasting System (later CBS), where he worked games for the next twenty years.

Husing is credited with inventing the annunciator board, a mechanical device first used in 1926 and in which Husing's assistant used binoculars to identify jersey numbers and then typed them onto a keyboard. The numbers corresponded to a player's name, which then flashed on for Husing to see.

Les Quailey joined Husing as a broadcasting partner in 1929.

At least one radio critic from the *New York Herald Tribune* favored Husing over McNamee:

"Husing has given more complete information, more accurate and prompt news of the changing position of the ball, and acute observations as to place, possibilities, and potentialities of the teams and individual players on the field before him than have either of the more noted announcers (McNamee and partner Carlin) ... Husing is likely to become radio's most appreciated football describer, unless, of course, Mr. McNamee and Mr. Carlin come close to realize that the primary purpose of a football broadcast is not to furnish verbal entertainment but to provide immediate news of what the twenty-two football players are doing."

A third noteworthy announcer during the McNamee-Husing era was Georgia native Bill Munday. The colorful Southerner was a popular play-by-play man until alcohol sidetracked his career. He did overcome that later in life, and wound up broadcasting Georgia Bulldog games.

By the 1940s, Husing's chief sportscasting rival was NBC's Bill Stern, a Rochester, New York, native. Stern worked in both radio and television, and, according to most, was best suited to the former.

"Stern's smooth voice, chatty presence, and knack for pulling out the right anecdote were far more suited to radio than television," according to *Play-by-Play*. "Stern also appeared more interested in telling a good story than in precise reporting, something more favorably received in radio, where listeners could not see if Stern was accurately describing the game."

Another well-known name was Harry Wismer, a Michigan native who called college and pro games for NBC and ABC for twenty years. He became heavily involved in ownership and management in the NFL with the Detroit Lions and Washington Redskins, but his eventual financial downfall came with his investment in the New York Titans in the AFL.

Several others came soon after, including Tennessee native Lindsey Nelson. He originally did Tennessee Volunteer football games and then became well known for broadcasting Notre Dame football, the Cotton Bowl game, and major league baseball.

And then, deep in the heart of Texas, there was Kern Tips.

The Houston native had studied at both Texas A&M and Rice; from 1924-34, he served as a sports reporter/editor at the *Houston Chronicle.*

His association with radio began in 1926, first as a sportscaster and later as a newscaster.

By 1935, when Humble came calling, Tips, a distinguished-looking gentleman with a distinguished voice, was general manager of radio station KPRC in Houston.

Tips did his first Humble broadcast—Rice vs. St. Mary's—on September 21, 1935, and, unlike sportswriter Lloyd Gregory, he was an immediate hit.

Dallas broadcaster Ves Box, who joined the Humble network in 1938, picks up the story from there, in *Texas Signs On:*

"Kern began broadcasting when Humble began broadcasting in 1936. Humble had been dabbling with it and used sports writers for announcers with some rather dire results, according to some of the stories I heard. Kern had been a sports writer ... and was widely followed as a young sports writer.... He was selected in 1935 or '36 by Humble to do some trial broadcasting for them and developed into their lead announcer. He was head and shoulders above anyone else. He was very particular about the people he worked with—in that they did their job. He had a wonderful vocabulary and could express himself eloquently; could see as much football as anybody, and tell more football, and tell it accurately. Some of us had a tendency to lag behind the play, but he was right up with it—had a great pair of eyes—never used field glasses."

Indeed, Tips appeared to be particular about who he chose as his number-two man in the booth—from 1934 to 1945, he "auditioned" more than twenty color announcers before settling on longtime partner Alec Chesser in 1946. Tips-Chesser remained a team for the next twenty years until Tips's death in 1967.

With Tips established as the lead announcer, the "Game of the Week" concept was established.

Former TCU football star Cy Leland served as the number-two play-by-play man from 1935-41; after that, Box assumed that role until the mid-1960s.

Each year, Humble-Enco-Exxon distributed free Southwest Conference football schedule cards and ads to service station customers. (courtesy of ExxonMobil)

By the late 1940s-early 1950s, Humble had also begun televising select SWC games, with Tips/Chesser frequently in the TV booth, while a separate crew was onsite doing radio.

"He had the fastest eye-voice coordination I've ever seen," recalled Bill Sansing in *The Golden Voices of Football*. "It was uncanny. Kern described it as fast as he saw it. There was no lag time. He didn't even need a spotter."

Sansing, who was the first full-time sports information director at the University of Texas in the 1940s before establishing a high-profile marketing career (clients included Jack Nicklaus and the Dallas Cowboys), said: "(Tips) had a deep, resonant voice. He could go anywhere in Texas, and people would recognize his voice after just a few words."

Tips was famous for his colorful sayings. According to the 2006 autobiography, *Eddie Barker's Notebook*, an individual named Billy Oxley did his master's thesis at the University of Texas in 1965. His topic? Kern Tips's play-by-play style.

Oxley noted that during the 1964 Texas-SMU game, Tips spoke an average of 232 words per minute.

Oxley added that Tips used precise nouns, bold adjectives, and forceful verbs.

"It was obvious that while Kern Tips had, and used, a number of standard words and phrases to describe the actions on the field, he also had developed a series of very colorful and descriptive phrases, which he used from time to time to give variety to his sportscast," Oxley noted. "The effect of his insertion of these colorful phrases into his descriptions led the listener to believe that his speech was really more colorful than it was."

When there was a fumble, Tips declared there was "a malfunction at the junction;" when a quarterback was sacked, "he had to peel it and eat it that time;" a long pass was "he pulls the trigger on the long ball;" a run gain in a night game was "he rumbles for a little moonlight;" and a kicker "lays leather to the ball."

At the same time, Tips was careful not to overdo each broadcast with too many clichés.

A 1954 press release distributed by Humble noted that Tips broadcast thirteen games a season, with the games averaging 2¾ hours in length or a total of 29¼ hours. The release went on to state that since Tips talks about 150 words a minute, he speaks some 264,250 words during a football season. And on top of that, not one word was scripted.

"A good many people believe he worked at these phrases," his longtime broadcasting partner Chesser once said. "They just came to him—often times they even surprised him. Kern never wrote those expressions down, they just happened."

Mike Shropshire, in his 2006 book, *Running with the Big Dogs*, reflected on the SWC glory days and the influence Tips had:

"On football Saturdays, Kern Tips would entertain the audience with his completely unique play-by-play poetry, the lilting and cheerful radio voice of the Southwest Conference radio network. . . In Kern Tips's audio world, placekickers didn't kick extra points— they made seven out of six. And those guys weren't diving for a loose football—they were playing "button, button—who's got the button?" And about once a quarter, somebody would run the "old dipsy-doodle." Nobody knew what that meant, but it sounded like a helluva lot. Everybody loved to listen to Kern Tips."

Verne Lundquist was a longtime college football/basketball television play-by-play man for ABC and CBS who retired in 2016. Lundquist, who first gained recognition as a sportscaster at WFAA-TV in Dallas while working Dallas Cowboys radio broadcasts, was a great admirer of Tips, as he related to the *Sports Business Journal* in 2014:

"He was the voice of my childhood. . . . I grew up listening to Tips. One of the great thrills I had was standing by his side on a broadcast and keeping his stats. Kern's phrases were legendary. He was very descriptive, used good adjectives, and was loved throughout

Texas. . . . He was wonderfully creative in his descriptive abilities."

Tom Hedrick called games for Exxon in 1973-74 while working as a Dallas sportscaster (KDFW) and recently retired after a sixty-two-year career in broadcasting. Although he never worked with Tips, Hedrick had the highest respect for the Voice of the Southwest Conference.

He listened to Tips's broadcasts and also had a chance to meet him on at least one occasion.

"I heard Kern Tips, and I thought he was fantastic," Hedrick said in 2019. "I loved his expressions. He was kind of understated, but he had a tremendous following."

Many would point to Tips as the forerunner to longtime national college football announcer Keith Jackson, who began his career in 1952 and was well-known for his folksy sayings.

Glenn Brown, an H/E/E announcer off-and-on from 1951-1977, also had high praise for Tips.

"In my opinion, no one will ever be better," Brown wrote on hornfans.com in 2007. "He coined many phrases that you still hear today. . . . I always wanted to be as good, but never was, of course. I wanted, like Kern, to paint a sound picture so that listeners could virtually see the game. . . . Kern Tips was the best who ever lived at his job."

Tee Casper, another former Humble announcer, had this to say in a 1985 interview with the *El Paso Times:*

"I worked before World War II with Kern Tips on the Southwest Conference broadcasts. Tips was good; while the rest of us were living it up, Tips was learning his teams and studying. He was the Humble network for a long time."

Connie Alexander, who became the network's lead play-by-play man in the mid-1960s, said in a 1970 interview with the *Associated Press*: "Kern Tips was famous for his extensive preparation. . . . Kern was an inspiration to me, as he was to any announcer who ever heard him."

And while broadcasters such as McNamee, Husing, Stern, Wismer, and Nelson might have been more recognizable on a national level, Tips was highly regarded by his peers, both near and far.

In particular, Nelson, who would become a broadcasting legend, readily recognized the ability of the Texan. After being praised for his own work in 1951 by a Texas radio general manager, Nelson turned the attention back to Tips.

"Everybody in Texas knew who the greatest football broadcaster in the whole world was," Nelson wrote in *Hello Everybody, I'm Lindsey Nelson*, his 1985 autobiography. "And I was not about to presume greatness beyond that conferred daily by the constituency of Kern Tips. Kern Tips had been the "voice" of southwest football for a lot of years, and to presume an encroachment would be self-destructive heresy. Kern and I would become close friends."

As the lead SWC announcer, Tips assigned crews to the weekly games. His career outside the radio booth also blossomed:

A Tribute to Kern Tips

Rolling Along With

Tumbleweed Smith

Ron Starry lives in Fredericksburg. Like many Texas boys who grew up in the fifties, many a Saturday afternoon he and some friends listened to Kern Tips describe the southwest conference football games. They listened to the car radio or on one of those new transistor jobs.

"I have memories of being in the middle of a hay meadow hunting doves and listening to Kern broadcast a game in 1960 between the Arkansas Razorbacks and the Texas Longhorns. They had Lance Alworth, we had Jimmy Saxton." Ron went to Texas.

He has many memories of listening to Kern Tips describe football games.

"He's obviously the best I ever heard and probably the best that ever was."

When the Southwest conference was splitting up, Ron was sitting out at the golf course one day with a friend talking about Kern Tips. "A poem began forming in my mind," says Ron. "About a year later I decided to write it down."

He sent it to a newspaper in San Antonio, which published the poem. "It really surprised me and pleased me. Many people have come up to me and thanked me for the poem and told me it touched them."

He has written poetry before, but "none of it very good," he says. "It's not my usual vocation." Ron is in real estate and raises Spanish goats. He owned and operated college bookstores for years and is now semi-retired.

The poem about Kern Tips goes like this:

I think I heard Kern Tips last night.
The voice was pure, but sad.
Was this really on my radio or just a dream I had?
My mind was fixed on Bobby and big John David Crow.
And I cried last night for old Kern tips, who died so long ago.
He must be at his microphone. He wants to turn it on.
"There's thunder up the middle, boys, looks like Dupre's long gone."
I wonder what he thinks of us, in that press box in the sky.
We who remain must share the blame. We let the conference die.
I know I heard Kern Tips last night.
The voice was strong and clear. It must have been the Cotton Bowl,
But I don't recall the year.
For a moment I was in the stands, turned up my radio.
And then I cried and cried for old Kern Tips
Who died so long ago.

The legacy of announcer Kern Tips is demonstrated by this newspaper column written by Tumbleweed Smith in 1997. (courtesy of Tumbleweed Smith)

He left KPRC on January 1, 1947, to join the advertising agency of Wilkinson-Schiwetz-Tips; in September, 1954, when the firm merged with McCann-Erickson, one of the world's largest advertising agencies, Tips became a vice president.

(McCann-Erickson is perhaps best known for developing the "Put a Tiger in Your Tank" ad campaign for Humble in 1964, and, in 1971, the "It's the Real Thing" slogan for Coca-Cola. Years later, the ad agency entered pop culture, playing a prominent role on the popular AMC television series, *Mad Men.)*

Even legendary CBS newsman Walter Cronkite was influenced by Tips, as he recalled in a 2009 interview with Don Carleton, executive director of the University of Texas at Austin's Dolph Briscoe Center for American History.

"I always was intrigued with radio, but I never really thought a lot about being a radio reporter," Cronkite said. "I remember when I was in Houston and still in high school, I became friendly with a guy named Kern Tips at KTRH radio, who became a radio legend in Texas, especially for his work as a sports announcer for the football broadcasts that the Humble Oil Company sponsored... Anyway, Kern Tips imitated Floyd Gibbons, who was famous nationally in those days as a radio announcer and movie newsreel narrator. He talked very rapidly. I don't know whether he learned it from Floyd Gibbons, but Kern pasted his script together in a scroll, so he wouldn't waste any time turning pages. He pasted the whole darn thing together on this long script they had on the floor and he stood at the microphone, and held this script along his fingers. I went down to watch him broadcast two or three times."

Of all the memorable games that Tips did, two stand out simply because of horrific weather.

On October 20, 1956, Texas A&M defeated No. 4 TCU, 7-6, in what was known as the "Hurricane Game." Rain and hail halted the game in the second quarter in College Station.

"More than 150 planes at Easterwood Airport were overturned, and the playing field became 100 yards of pig slop," according to *Pride in Aggieland.*

And on September 18, 1965, the Kansas-Texas Tech game at Jones Stadium in Lubbock was stopped in the fourth quarter after torrential rain, high winds, and tornadoes pummeled the area. Tips and Chesser signed off the air with Tech leading, 26-7.

In 1964, Tips authored an impressive book entitled *Football Texas Style—An Illustrated History of the Southwest Conference.* Upon retiring from the ad agency in 1966, he produced and narrated a syndicated series of five-minute sports radio shows broadcast throughout the Southwest. And he continued to produce and narrate Humble's "Southwest Conference Highlights," an annual film recapping the previous season and shown throughout the state at civic clubs and various gatherings.

Tips's voice was beamed around the world through the facilities of the Armed Forces Radio Service Network. He served as a member of the board of directors of the National Association of Broadcasters from 1939-40, as an advisor to the Office of War Information during World War II, and as director of Civilian Defense for Houston and Harris County from 1943-45.

In 1959, Tips was selected as the man who had contributed the most to radio and television in Texas by receiving the first award presented by the Association of Broadcasting Executives in Texas. He was also the recipient of the only award ever presented by the Southwest Football Officials Association for distinguished service to the sport.

And Tips was voted Texas Sportscaster of the Year five consecutive years. He was inducted into the Texas Sports Hall of Fame in 2005.

Tips broadcast his last game on December 17, 1966, at Rice Stadium in Houston (Bluebonnet Bowl, Ole Miss vs. Texas).

Due to declining health, he had not planned on broadcasting any games in 1967; Tips died of cancer on August 3, 1967, at Methodist Hospital in Houston at age sixty-two, survived by his wife, Nancy, and two children. He had been hospitalized since July 17.

In 1968, the Humble Oil & Refining Company announced the Kern Tips Memorial Trophy would be awarded to an outstanding Southwest Conference senior football player each year.

But while Tips had achieved fame, he remained a bit of an enigma, according to those who knew him. That included Eddie Barker, who broadcast games on the Humble network from 1947-62. In fact, Barker worked side-by-side in the booth with Tips on six games in 1954.

In *Eddie Barker's Notebook*, he recalled a couple of Tips's idiosyncrasies: "He was a Christian Scientist, but carried a flask of whiskey and took a little nip after the game. He always stacked multiple chairs to sit on during the game, so he'd be sitting at an angle tilting forward as he looked at the field."

Another source suggested that Tips, because of a reluctance to travel, did an inordinate number of Rice games in Houston, where he resided.

Wrote Barker:

"I think a lot of fans in those days would rather listen to Kern describe a game on radio than see the game in person. He was that good. . . . He was the best at what he did. But I often wonder if anyone ever really knew the man."

TOEING THE COMPANY LINE

Each summer, in preparation for the upcoming football season, Kern Tips and his crew of announcers went back to "school."

At these planning sessions, originated by Tips, the announcers were joined by various Southwest Conference coaches and officials.

"The main purpose of the school was to get back to the fundamentals of football," Tips commented after the 1954 gathering, which featured University of Texas coach Ed Price and his staff. "We just wanted to review all rule changes and basic football plays to try and make our broadcasts more interesting."

After Coach Price's presentation, Tips reviewed the practices used in broadcasts of the games.

"Never editorialize," he told the announcers. "Just report what is happening and remember, teams are penalized, not individuals, even though the

Humble's Football Announcers Prepare For Exciting Season

FORT WORTH—Humble's outstanding staff of football announcers met recently in Fort Worth to discuss plans for the 1957 season, and to get better acquainted with coaches and officials of the Southwest. This friendly association has resulted through the years in the fullest cooperation and understanding between Humble, the announcers, and the schools of the Southwest.

Shown at right is Abe Martin, left, head coach of Texas Christian University, describing a play for Kern Tips, dean of Humble's announcers and a describer of games without peer.

AWAITING ACTION—Relaxed now, these ten men will soon be much more solemn when they begin reporting exciting football action of the Southwest. These men make up Humble's renowned broadcasting staff, headed by Kern Tips, center, front row. A top-flight announcer must be on his toes every minute during an action-packed game of the Southwest. These men have proved that they can do just that and give colorful word pictures that approximate the live action.

"We will be your partner in sales," say the smiling group, standing, l. to r., Eddie Barker, Jim Wiggins, John Phelan, Alec Chesser, Connie Alexander, Eddie Hill, and Dave Russel. Front row shows Bob Walker, Tips, and Ves Box.

Over the years, Humble created awareness of its radio coverage of SWC games in a number of ways. For example, the company produced news releases and photographs for Texas newspapers and other publications, including this promotional piece prior to the 1957 season. (courtesy of ExxonMobil)

foul may be personal. And always remember to emphasize team play. No one player makes the touchdown. He couldn't do it if the whole team didn't play together."

Indeed, by today's standards of "telling it like it is"—to quote the late Howard Cosell—Humble's rules were rather archaic but apparently not that unusual for the times.

And it should be noted that during this time, Humble's announcers were not alone in "promoting" the sport.

According to *Play-by-Play*, "Radio and television announcers for college athletics played the publicity game much as did college presidents—principally glorifying the positive aspects of the game and ignoring the negative ones. College football was often thought to be the apex for an announcer's career. The college game, after all, was played by amateur student-athletes on bucolic Saturday afternoons among teams of friendly strife. Announcers, first on radio, and then on television, were expected to depict that scene. For the most part, the golden voices did just that. From Bill Stern to Lindsey Nelson to Keith Jackson, the announcers promoted a rosy picture of college sport to a receptive American public."

Furthermore, as Michael Oriard writes in *King Football*, the role of the college football broadcaster in the 1930s was much different than what we are accustomed to today.

"Early radio broadcasts assumed a different function," according to Oriard. "More simply, to recreate for listeners the experience of being at the game. Much more so than baseball, college football games were staged in settings that mattered as much as the games themselves. The crowds, the bands, the card sections, the cheerleaders—the endlessly noted "spirit" of college football—were crucial to football's appeal, and thus to the announcers who tried to capture it."

Rule number one for Humble announcers: Be objective and unbiased in calling the game. This, of course, is just the opposite of today's standards, in that most major schools have their own radio networks and employ their own announcers who espouse rather biased commentary.

Dave Smith, who handled color duties on H/E/E from 1951-77, told Texas newspaper columnist Tumbleweed Smith in a 1990 interview that "we never covered the same team two weeks in a row to avoid us being called 'homers' and becoming partial to that particular team."

"You were not a homer," said longtime (1955-77) H/E/E color announcer Stan McKenzie in *Texas Signs On*. "You were nonbiased. They did not like to get criticism that this announcer liked this team or that team."

And if an announcer violated these rules, McKenzie said, "He was gone." (See *Eddie Barker and the Rest Is History*, Chapter 7.)

Jack Dale, who broadcast games on the network for twenty-five years, beginning in the mid-1950s, said in an interview with the *Houston Chronicle*, "it was pure and simple reporting. You did the play-by-play, and the color man would do his bit and read the commercials."

Dave South, in a 2017 interview with David Barron of the *Chronicle*, and who joined the H/E/E broadcast team during its final few years, said, "Exxon was pretty restrictive. You showed no favoritism, even if a Southwest Conference team was playing a non-conference opponent. You had to be excited for both sides. They figured that if LSU was playing A&M, there would be some LSU fans listening. I was told that Exxon would get credit cards cut in half with a note saying, 'I don't like what your announcers said about my team,' so they were very cautious."

Another cardinal rule was to never describe injuries or say if a player had been removed from a game due to an injury.

One story has it that when Southern California running back O. J. Simpson suffered cramps during a 1967 game with Texas, Humble announcers were not allowed to discuss his absence.

This is another example of Humble promoting its broadcasts of SWC football in newspapers throughout Texas. (courtesy of ExxonMobil)

MAKING PLANS — Humble Football announcers Kern Tips, left, and Alec Chesser, right, discuss radio broadcasts plans with Howard Grubbs (center), executive secretary of the Southwest Conference. The Humble Company has sponsored radio broadcasts of Southwest Conference games for the last 28 years. This year's first broadcasts can be heard Saturday, September 23.

Humble distributed photos like this one from 1961 for use in newspapers to help advertise its radio broadcasts. (courtesy of ExxonMobil)

"The people who ran the network felt that if Grandma heard on the radio that her grandson had been injured, it might cause her to have a stroke," South told the *Chronicle*. "They had their own way of doing things."

Ironically, H/E/E was broadcasting the 1971 TCU-Baylor game at which Horned Frogs Coach Jim Pittman suffered a fatal heart attack on the sidelines. The radio crew was not allowed to mention Pittman's collapse or death, but Fort Worth radio station WBAP cut into the broadcast to report the breaking news.

Dan Lovett, who worked Humble games from 1966-70 before joining the ABC network in New York, recalled the no-injury edict in a 2019 interview:

"I remember sitting in a meeting with several of the announcers, and Kern Tips made it clear that we were not to talk about injured football players. That's the one thing I remember about him. They pounded that into us. . . . I thought it was kind of backwards, but I never got into a discussion with Kern about it. But it was discussed occasionally among the announcing crews. I do remember a McCann (McCann-Erickson ad agency, which represented Humble throughout its sponsorship of SWC football) ad rep telling me that we didn't want to ever provide any information to alarm a family member."

Former H/E/E broadcaster Tom Hedrick expressed similar thoughts in a 2019 interview, saying, "I thought it was too strict, but I abided by it. I do think today we're (sportscasters) too dramatic and not as good as reporters as during the Kern Tips era."

In one instance, Tips was broadcasting a game when a section of the stadium's stands collapsed. Emergency sirens screamed in the background, but Tips never mentioned the situation.

While instructed not to report any action off the field, H/E/E announcers were also forbidden to criticize the officiating, second-guess a coach, mention a fight, or identify a player who was penalized.

Other rules: the school songs were always broadcast prior to kickoff; the bands were heard during halftime; there were few, if any, interviews; and the score was mentioned frequently. In fact, a representative from the McCann agency was stationed in the booth with a piece of paper labeled with "score" in big letters. Every few minutes he held it in front of the announcer to remind him it was time to relay the score to listeners.

And, according to Smith, an Austin advertising-public relations executive, "the broadcasters had to be in the booth by 9 a.m. Saturday for a 1 p.m. kickoff. If the game started at 8 p.m., the announcers were in the booth by 4 p.m. And the announcer, color man, producer, engineer, and spotters stayed together until the game was over. Alcohol was absolutely forbidden before, during and immediately after the game."

And one last thing that is certainly different from today—there was limited commercial interruption.

"It was a public relations thing for Humble rather than a money-making thing," McKenzie told *Texas Signs On*. "I think we had twelve commercials during the entire game. In the early days, if you had a commercial scheduled for the first quarter and there were no timeouts, you did not make up for that—'Scratch it.'"

Chesser, in an interview with the *Houston Post* in the late 1970s, said: "The Southwest Conference insisted that every game be carried. We set up the format and the coverage, and followed their guidelines. You always heard the bands at halftime, no interviews. . . . Kern had scheduling control. If it was a big intersectional game involving an SWC team against a lesser game involving two SWC teams, Kern opted for the conference game. That always made the SWC happy."

Whatever the case, it proved to be a successful formula: A 1960 Humble survey revealed that 2 million people listened/watched a game presented on the Humble network. That included 1.3 million men and 700,000 women.

THE VOICE OF THE
SOUTHWEST CONFERENCE II

At the tender age of ten, Weldon Connie Alexander was already being recognized for his public-speaking ability.

It was circa 1940, and Alexander was competing in the Texas Interscholastic League declamation contest for the tiny Moran schools. (Moran was a west Texas community with a population of less than a thousand—then and now.)

"It was a contest in which you'd recite a poem," Alexander recalled. "If you won the contest at your school, you'd move on to the county meet. If you won there, you'd move on to the district contest, and so forth on to the state level. When I was ten years old, I participated in some of those competitions and won a few ribbons."

Connie Alexander, center, is shown at work in the broadcast booth at a SWC game. (courtesy of Connie Alexander Play-by-Play Sports Broadcasting Collection, Center for Southwest Research & Special Collections, University of New Mexico)

That early success, coupled with his interest in athletics, eventually culminated in a star (announcer) being born.

But first things first.

The Alexander family moved to Albuquerque, New Mexico, when Connie was seventeen.

When quizzed one day by an Albuquerque High School bookkeeping teacher about his career ambition, Connie replied, "I think I'd like to be a sports announcer."

That same year, he landed his first job as a public address announcer for the Albuquerque Dukes minor league baseball team. It was a paid public-speaking job—two dollars a game—and the official start of his announcing career.

Alexander then entered the University of New Mexico as a speech and journalism major. At UNM, he had voice training, was a member of the debate team, and played on the Lobos baseball team.

From there, Alexander continued paying his dues, beginning his radio career in 1948 at age nineteen, working local high school football and basketball games at KVER in Albuquerque. By 1949-50, Alexander, now twenty, had begun broadcasting University of New Mexico Lobos basketball games and minor league baseball.

The young announcer's career was then interrupted by a four-year stint in the Air Force, but he returned to earn his UNM degree in 1955.

Alexander got a break when he joined up with Humble Oil to broadcast New Mexico Lobos football games. One thing led to another, and, by 1962, he was invited to join the Humble-Enco SWC team.

After just a couple of years of broadcasting SWC games, Alexander found himself being assigned more and more big games,

During pre-game activities, Connie Alexander poses next to "Big Bertha" – the bass drum of the University of Texas band. (courtesy of Connie Alexander Play-by-Play Sports Broadcasting Collection, Center for Southwest Research & Special Collections, University of New Mexico)

Exxon lead announcer Connie Alexander greets Texas Tech mascot Raider Red prior to kickoff of the October 29, 1977, game against the Texas Longhorns in Austin. (courtesy of Connie Alexander Play-by-Play Sports Broadcasting Collection, Center for Southwest Research & Special Collections, University of New Mexico)

many times the second-best game behind top announcer Kern Tips.

And upon the death of Tips in August of 1967, Alexander inherited the role as lead play-by-play announcer on Humble's SWC radio network.

Following in the footsteps of such a giant was a formidable challenge, but Alexander was up to the task, serving in that capacity for the final ten years of the network's existence.

Alexander's excited, dramatic, rapid-fire delivery, complete with clichés, captivated listeners, much like Tips had for so many years.

For Alexander, a loud crowd was a "Vesuvius of voices;" a low kick was, a "quail-high kickoff;" a long way to go for a first down was "It's third down and about a geography class to go;" several penalty flags were, "flags fell like autumn leaves;" a fumble, borrowing from Tips was, "a malfunction at the junction;" and listening to the band, was "Now down to the orchestra pit."

"I developed a library of descriptions, twenty-five categories, to add variety and unique trademark expressions," Alexander stated in a 2015 oral history interview with the Texas Tech Southwest Collection/Special Collections Library.

Fellow announcer Tom Hedrick, who worked several Cotton Bowl games on CBS Radio alongside Alexander, noted in his book (*The Art of Sportscasting*) that his friend had "180-200 expressions that he wanted to use in his broadcasts. He would post them on a wall and cross them off as he used them, and then recycle."

"I came on (the air) fired up and tried to maintain that tempo for the entire game," Alexander recalled in a 1979 interview with Jim Ferguson of the *Lubbock Avalanche-Journal.* "It was easy to do, too. I could get wrapped up in the excitement of the stadium alone. I lived to feel that excitement growing. So I would get to the game three hours before kickoff and walk around the field."

Jim Garner, who served as TCU sports information director in the early 1970s, once said, "Connie attacks a game like no one I've ever seen. Of all the play-by-play announcers I've worked with, he is the only one who goes to so much trouble to get ready for a game."

But Alexander was about much more than just clichés, he was truly a play-by-play innovator. For example, he developed a manual of preparation procedures at the game site and in the radio booth; he created a unique magnetic spotting system with an information tag for each player; he expanded spotter's duties and hand signals; he watched game film with one of the assistant coaches each week; and he studied the rules intensely, sometimes visiting with officials in their dressing room during pre-game.

In addition to all of that, he did speech exercises, pulling words from the diaphragm instead of his throat. And while he was aboard a plane flying to each week's game, Alexander reviewed a list of his colorful expressions for future use. (On Friday afternoons, Alexander would leave his job at Albuquerque Federal Savings & Loan and fly to do a game.)

His ultimate goal was to provide listeners with a clear picture of the game and to make his description of the game entertaining.

Finally, on the day after a broadcast, he would listen to a recording to critique his performance.

While Tips relied primarily on one right-hand man (Chesser) in the booth, Alexander, in most cases, split those duties between veteran H/E/E sidekicks Stan McKenzie and Dave Smith.

Alexander's most memorable broadcast was the December 6, 1969, "Game of the Century" or "Big Shootout" in Fayetteville between unbeaten Texas and Arkansas, attended by President Richard Nixon. He also was the radio voice of the Cotton Bowl and Sun Bowl for many years on CBS radio, and did a few NFL games as well.

Following Tips's death, Alexander took over the duties as narrator of the popular H/E/E "Southwest Conference Highlights" film.

In addition to his SWC duties, Alexander was the "Voice of the Western Athletic Conference" on NBC and TVS for basketball.

The end of Alexander's association with the SWC broadcasts coincided with Exxon ending its sponsorships of the games following the 1977 season.

Like Tips, Alexander earned numerous awards throughout his broadcasting career (1947-2011). He received four National Sportscasters Association awards, the Texas Sportscaster of the Year award, and three New Mexico Sportscaster of the Year awards. He is a member of the New Mexico Sports Hall of Fame.

In 2010-11, Alexander broadcast two seasons of Lobo baseball on radio 101.7 FM the TEAM (KQTM) in Albuquerque. All told, his broadcasting career spanned more than sixty-five years (1947-2011).

Alexander has ensured that his legacy will live on, having donated 173 recordings (reel-to-reel tapes and audio cassettes) of his work to two major universities. The "Connie Alexander Play-by-

Play Broadcasting Collection" is now available at the University of New Mexico Libraries Center for Southwest Research and Special Collections and the Texas Tech University Southwest Collection/ Special Collections Library.

"It's about love, loving my listeners, being a servant to them, creating a picture of the games in their minds," Alexander said in 2016 of his career.

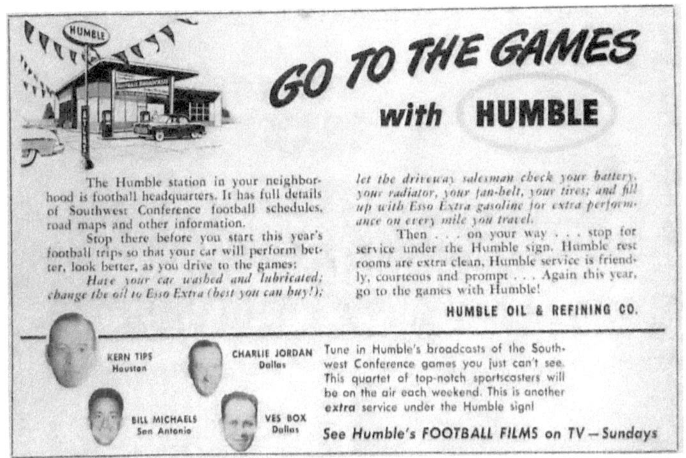

OTHER VOICES

While Kern Tips and Connie Alexander were the two most renowned Humble play-by-play announcers, other voices in the booth also distinguished themselves in a variety of ways.

Remember, with rare exceptions, the announcers were faceless to us; other than a few who did occasional TV work, we had no idea what most of them looked like.

Each announcing crew was comprised of a play-by-play man and a second individual who served as sort of a host announcer. And their roles were clearly defined. Filling out the booth were an engineer, producer, a couple of spotters, and, in the early days at least, a representative from the McCann- Erickson ad agency.

As previously outlined, the play-by-play man followed the strict guidelines imposed by Humble to objectively

FOOTBALL FANS throughout Texas know the voices of this quartet of announcers heard on Southwest Conference football broadcasts sponsored by the Humble Oil & Refining Company. Top, left, is Kern Tips, whose reputation is national in scope; experts agree that Tips is one of the best football announcers in the country—many say the best. Next to Tips, on the right, is all-America Cy Leland, who brings to broadcasting not only an ability to make a radio football game lively and interesting but also a knowledge of the game acquired by stellar play in the T. C. U. backfield in his college days. Bottom, right, is the picture of Hal Thompson, Station WFAA's sports authority; this is his third year on Humble's broadcasts. Flanking Thompson is Eddie Dunn, genial and well known radio personality who entered his second year on the Humble Company's football broadcasts this season.

Shown are two more examples of press releases and photos produced and distributed by Humble in marketing its broadcasts of Southwest Conference football.

These releases were published by Texas newspapers in 1938-39.
(courtesy of ExxonMobil)

and matter-of-factly describe the game with no editorial comments or observations.

Meanwhile, the second man in the booth handled a scripted opening, which had to be approved by a representative of McCann-Erickson (which produced the games), end-of-quarter commercials, statistics, halftime, and a scripted ending. In other words, no real "analysis" of the game as such.

And while some of the national radio networks employed former football stars such as Red Grange (NBC in the 1950s) and Tom Harmon (CBS in the 1950s, in addition to other networks later) to broadcast games, Humble, with rare exceptions—Cy Leland, for one—did not hire former star athletes.

Prior to his announcing career, Leland, who was from Lubbock, was a prolific athlete at Texas Christian University. He was an all-conference halfback on the Horned Frogs' 1929 unbeaten Southwest Conference team; at the 1930 Kansas Relays, he tied the world record in the 100-yard dash with a time of 9.4 seconds.

But in most cases, Humble employed little-known professional announcers or those working in a related field.

The Humble broadcasters came from a variety of backgrounds, with the most common being radio, news, public relations, and advertising. Many of them were versatile enough to handle either role of play-by-play or color, and many of them went on to storied careers in broadcasting, entertainment, or the business world.

With a few exceptions, most of the broadcasters were based in Texas—the vast majority from Dallas-Fort Worth or Houston.

Prior to his announcing career, Cy Leland of Lubbock was a prolific athlete at Texas Christian University. (courtesy of TCU Athletics)

Leland served essentially as the No. 2 play-by-play man behind Tips from 1935-41.

Another longtime Humble broadcaster was Ves Box, who called games from 1938-1967, and assumed the number-two role after Leland's departure. Box was the chief announcer at KRLD Radio in Dallas, and eventually became president of KRLD/KDFW (Channel 4) in Dallas.

Alec Chesser was the best-known color announcer, deftly handling the duties as right-hand man for twenty-four seasons (1944-67), most of that time alongside Tips. All told, he worked 270 broadcasts for Humble. Chesser was also successful as a radio announcer/newsman in Cincinnati and San Antonio, and he later became an account executive with McCann-Erickson in Houston. Still later, Chesser served as vice president of the Houston Natural Gas Corporation.

Jerry Doggett, in above photo at right, handled both play-by-play and color duties on Humble SWC football games from 1944-56, and later worked for Gordon McLendon's Liberty Broadcasting System. But he is most recognized for his 32-year career as Vin Scully's (in above photo with Doggett) sidekick on Brooklyn and Los Angeles Dodgers' major league broadcasts. (courtesy of Los Angeles Dodgers Baseball Club)

THE FACES
BEHIND THE VOICES

Connie Alexander

Eddie Barker

Buddy Bostick

Ves Box

Conrad Brady

Alec Chesser

Jack Dale

Jerry Doggett

Eddie Dunn

Gene Elston

Frank Fallon

John Ferguson

Pat Flaherty

Eddie Gallaher

Frank Glieber

Lloyd Gregory

Tom Hedrick

Bill Hightower

Bob Holton

Bill Karn

Cy Leland

Dan Lovett

Stan McKenzie

Fred Nahas

Bob Nash

John Phelan

Byrum Saam

Guy Savage

Hal Thompson

Kern Tips

Jim Wiggins

San Antonio advertising executive Jim Wiggins had one of the longest tenures as a Humble-Enco-Exxon announcer, working SWC games from 1949-77. (Author's collection)

Southwest Conference Football: a team effort.

As the nine schools of the Southwest Conference compete for that coveted berth in the Cotton Bowl, individual team effort and commitment is essential. Players, coaches, students, alumni, fans. Pulling together for a common goal.

And there's another all-important team…the men who bring you all the action every week on the Exxon Football Network. Dedicated, experienced broadcast veterans who call all the drama, color, and excitement of Southwest Conference Football in such a way that's the next best thing to being there. This 1976 season marks the 43rd consecutive year of these thrilling broadcasts sponsored by Exxon. We welcome the University of Houston as an active competitor in Southwest Conference Football, and are proud to be broadcasting their full schedule of games for the first time.

Support your favorite team by attending as many games as you can. But when you can't, tune in the play-by-play on your radio. Then, in December, watch for the presentation of the annual Kern Tips Award to the outstanding senior student/athlete.

It's all part of Southwest Conference Football, 1976. We hope you enjoy it.

In 1976, Exxon placed ads in various publications promoting its SWC broadcasting team. (courtesy of ExxonMobil)

Jerry Doggett, a Dallas radio broadcaster, handled both duties for Humble from 1944-56. He also worked for Gordon McLendon's Liberty Broadcasting System before embarking on a thirty-two-year career as Vin Scully's sidekick on Brooklyn and Los Angeles Dodgers' major league broadcasts.

Bill Michaels was general manager of San Antonio radio station KABC, and did play-by-play for Humble from 1941-53. He later (1966) became president of Storer Broadcasting, and he then served as CEO and chairman of the board there until his retirement.

Charlie Jordan, who worked Humble games from 1942-1952, operated Fort Worth radio station KFJZ and the Texas State Network.

Baton Rouge's John Ferguson broadcast SWC games for just four years (1951-54), but later became recognized as the voice of the LSU Tigers for thirty years.

Buddy Bostick provided color work from 1939-50, founded Waco TV station KWTX, and later owned stations in Bryan, Sherman, and Lafayette (Louisiana). He also was a bank executive in Waco.

In addition to Tips, Box, and Chesser, those broadcasters with the longest tenure with H/E/E were San Antonio advertising executive Jim Wiggins (1949-77), who also hosted a popular live country music show and did play-by-play for the San Antonio Missions minor league baseball team; Eddie Hill of Dallas (1951-77); Austin advertising/public relations man Dave Smith (1951-77); Lubbock radio broadcaster Jack Dale (1953-77); Glenn Brown of Austin (off and on from 1951-77); Seguin radio station executive Stan McKenzie (1955-77); John Smith, a Memphis, Tennessee, advertising/public relations executive, (1957-77); and Beaumont-Dallas radio broadcaster Dave Russell (off and on from 1940-61).

Fort Worth native Byrum "By" Saam did a few Humble games in 1935; he eventually become nationally known as the first voice of Philadelphia baseball, broadcasting games for the Phillies and

Athletics, and also worked professional football, basketball, and hockey games.

Eddie Gallaher of Tulsa worked a couple of games on the Humble network in 1937. He earned fame in Washington, D.C., calling Washington Redskins' football games and as a longtime music and radio broadcaster.

At least eight Humble announcers—Harfield Weedin, Dan Riss, Bob Holton, Bill Karn, Rudy Tellez, Ray Cullin, Fort Pearson, and Eddie Barker (see Chapter 7, *Eddie Barker and the Rest Is History*) went on to achieve notoriety in the news reporting, television, or motion picture business.

Weedin, who began his radio career while a student at the University of Texas at Austin, called Humble games from 1938-43, partnering with Tips on a number of occasions. Lady Bird Johnson had hired him during this time to serve as general manager of her radio station (KTBC) in Austin. After serving in the Navy at Armed Forces Radio Service in Hollywood, Weedin worked for ABC, where he wrote such popular shows as *Abbott and Costello* and *Meet Corliss Archer*, and produced Groucho Marx's *You Bet Your Life* television show. In 1958, he co-produced Ralph Edwards's *End of the Rainbow* on NBC television. In 1961, he moved to KNX radio, and later served as director of programming for the CBS Radio Network until his retirement in 1982.

Dan Riss, who was born in Illinois, had a unique career, calling games for the Florida Gators in the late 1930s. He described games on the Humble network from 1939-42, while holding positions at radio stations in Dallas and then Cincinnati. Riss then decided to try his luck in Hollywood, and enjoyed an acting career in movies and television that lasted from 1949-1965. Among his movie credits were *Pinky, Panic in the Streets,* and *Appointment with Danger*. He also appeared as a guest on numerous popular TV shows, including *Bonanza, Wagon Train, Perry Mason, Dragnet, The Lone Ranger, Death Valley Days,* and *Gunsmoke.*

Gene Elston was best-known as the play-by-play man for the Houston Astros baseball team from 1962-86, but he also worked Southwest Conference football games on the Exxon network in 1976-77. (courtesy of Houston Astros Baseball Club)

Dallas native Robert Wilson Holton graduated from the University of Texas at Austin with a degree in speech and drama and worked at WFAA Radio in Dallas. In 1943, he did color on a couple of games on the Humble network. He wound up in Hollywood, and was best known for having portrayed Jesus in several movies in the 1950s, including *Family Theatre: I Beheld His Glory*, *The Living Christ Series* (a twelve-episode film series), and also on stage in *The Pilgrimage Play*.

Karn, who was born in Tucumcari, New Mexico, handled color duties on a handful of Humble broadcasts in 1940-41. His varied career included stops at JC Penney; radio stations in Pampa (KPDN), Cincinnati, and Oklahoma City; advertising; the U.S. Army; and, finally, Hollywood. He enjoyed a prolific time as a TV-movie director-producer-writer in the 1950s and early 1960s.

Among the motion pictures he was involved with were *Ma Barker's Killer Brood*, *Five Minutes to Live*, and *Guns Don't Argue*. Karn's TV credits included *Gang Busters*, *Schlitz Playhouse*, and *Dangerous Assignment*.

Tellez, an El Paso native, began his career at local station KTSM as a radio producer and on-air personality. He was the number-two announcer with El Paso broadcasting icon John Phelan on the 1957 Humble broadcast of the Texas Tech-Texas Western game. Tellez produced talk show host Les Crane in the early 1960s in San Francisco for KGO, and later produced such programs as *The Tomorrow Show* with Tom Snyder, *The Wacky World of Jonathan Winters*, and *The Battle of the Network Stars*. But he was best known for producing *The Tonight Show* with Johnny Carson during a four-year period (1968-71), for which he was nominated for two Emmy awards.

Also distinguishing himself nationally was Ray Cullin, a TV/radio broadcaster in Lubbock and Amarillo, who called a handful of Humble games in 1955. Cullin then went to work for NBC News in Burbank, Calif., and retired after more than thirty-three years as a correspondent, show producer, political field producer, bureau chief, White House producer, and West Coast producer for NBC *Nightly News*. During his time at NBC, Cullin covered nine presidents and every election from 1968-2000.

And a man with a most intriguing name—Fort Pearson—did play-by-play on a few of the early Humble games in the mid-1930s. He also did the NBC radio college football game of the week; later, he became well-known as the announcer on such radio shows as *The Guiding Light* and *Queen for a Day*, touting such products as PandG Naphtha Soap and Alka-Seltzer.

Glenn Brown had an interesting career outside the radio booth. A graduate of the University of Texas School of Law, Brown worked, at various times, in the following capacities: Austin sports TV anchor, Texas assistant attorney general, appointed by President

Lyndon Johnson to head the Small Business Investment Company in Washington D.C., and as a travel advance man overseas for LBJ. He retired in 2009 as president of the Dairy Products Institute of Texas.

Other familiar names handling play-by-play/color duties on the H/E/E network in the late 1960s and early 1970s were legendary Waco radio man Frank Fallon, former Houston Oilers announcer, later the voice of the Baylor Bears and SWC basketball on TV, and longtime public address announcer for the NCAA Final Four; Dan Lovett, a Houston sportscaster who later worked for the ABC network; and Gene Elston, the well-respected veteran play-by-play man of the Houston Astros, who joined the Exxon team in 1976 when the University of Houston became a member of the Southwest Conference.

Probably the most famous name to take the second chair was radio legend Gordon McLendon, who worked a few Humble games in the late 1940s. Known as "the Old Scotsman" and "the Maverick of Radio," McLendon founded the Liberty Radio Network in the 1940s, one of the nation's largest networks, which carried Major League Baseball games as well as studio-recreated games. He is credited by most broadcast historians with having established the first mobile news units in American radio, the first traffic reports, the first jingles, the first all-news radio station, the first "easy-listening" programming, and he was among the first to popularize the top 40 radio format and to utilize innovative and off-the-wall promotions.

At the age of twenty-four, Milwaukee native Frank Glieber made his Humble debut in 1958 in the color booth. He went on to a distinguished career as a Dallas sportscaster and CBS broadcaster, most notably in pro football and golf.

Also frequently serving in the role of color announcer was Lubbock TV sportscaster Ray Boyd (1965-77) and Mike Mistovich (off and on from 1954-72), a former minor league baseball pitcher from Virginia and who was a longtime basketball voice of the Texas Aggies and Bryan radio station owner.

The previously mentioned Dave Smith and Stan McKenzie became fixtures alongside Connie Alexander, the network's top play-by-play man for ten years following the death of Tips and after the retirement of Chesser.

Alexander's on-air enthusiasm was such that he would often throw the mic to McKenzie and proclaim, "And now, here's Stan the Man!"

Most listeners will recall that the typical color announcer exuded a warm, kind and friendly manner, which complemented his play-by-play partner in the booth.

RECREATING STORIES FROM THE BOOTH

One name synonymous with Baylor Bears athletics and broadcasting is that of Frank Fallon.

Known as a consummate professional, Fallon spent more than forty years describing the action of Baylor football and basketball games and Texas high school football games. He also did Houston Oilers games, in addition to his NCAA Final Four responsibilities.

Although Fallon called a number of memorable contests over the years, the date of October 26, 1974, will always be remembered. It was on that day at Legion Field in Birmingham, Alabama, that TCU running back Kent Waldrep suffered a paralyzing injury. Again, due to network guidelines, Exxon radio announcers Fallon and Gene Arnold were not allowed to talk about the injury to listeners.

Frank Fallon was a fixture on the Southwest broadcasting scene for more than forty years and would eventually be known as the "Voice of the Baylor Bears." (courtesy of John Morris, Baylor Athletics)

Fallon's career also included television play-by-play of Southwest Conference basketball games for NBC and ESPN, a twenty-nine-year stint as general manager of KWTX Radio in Waco, and more than a decade as Baylor's coordinator of broadcast activities. In addition, Fallon mentored many Baylor telecommunications students and future play-by-play announcers through courses he taught from 1984 until his retirement in 1995.

Fallon died in 2004.

"He was the best there ever was," said John Morris, who replaced Fallon at Baylor and is the current voice of the Bears. "We worked together for eight years (SWC and Baylor games), and he was my mentor. He had such a great voice, but his preparation was what set him apart. And I learned so much just from the way he carried himself."

Tom Hedrick, a former H/E/E announcer, echoes those thoughts.

"Frank Fallon was one of my best friends," Hedrick said. "And he had such a marvelous voice."

Fallon was born in El Paso, but grew up in San Antonio, where he took a job at KITE in 1948. Five years later, he joined KWTX in Waco. And while he began broadcasting Baylor games in 1953, he was a latecomer to the H/E/E team, joining in circa 1970 and doing games through the end of the network in 1977. After that, he continued broadcasting SWC games on the Mutual and Host networks and then eventually on Baylor's own network.

According to family members (he and his wife had four sons), Frank Fallon's thorough preparation began early each day at home.

"I remember he used to get up at 5:30 in the morning and go out in the front yard and get four newspapers," son Mike recalled. "Then he would come in the house, take out all the sports sections, and read them from cover to cover."

As a teenager, Mike would travel to many of the games with his father.

"He took me to a lot of games—we'd leave early Saturday morning and drive in his '65 Ford," Mike said. "I would sit in the press box—my job was to take a transmitter to the locker room to set up for Dad for the post-game interviews."

Another Fallon son, Steve, also went to some games with his dad, but in a different role as a side-by-side color announcer on the Mutual network. But that pairing didn't last long, according to Steve, who later enjoyed a long career as executive director of the Texas Sports Hall of Fame in Waco.

"They said our voices sounded too much alike, so they separated us," he said. "I was flattered by that—it was a compliment to me, but Dad didn't like it."

Unlike many other play-by-play announcers, Fallon did not rely on others or utilize an elaborate spotter system with magnets and charts in the radio booth. Instead, he relied on one person—himself.

"He never used spotters—he memorized the first and second teamers and used binoculars," Mike said. "He also had a three-minute hour glass that he would turn over to remind himself to give the score and time throughout the game."

Morris concurs, recalling the eight years they shared in the booth.

"I remember he had two rosters in front of him on a clipboard," Morris said. "And that was it."

During his H/E/E days, Fallon did play-by-play with a rotating cast of color announcers.

"Dad always liked working with (Seguin radio station executive) Stan McKenzie," Steve said. "He was a good guy, who always prepared well. And he and Dave South were very close, having worked together (at KWTX) for many years in Waco."

South, who was from Wichita Falls, joined H/E/E in 1970. He would later become well-known as the "Voice of the Texas Aggies" and is the last former Exxon announcer still doing games. At age seventy-two, he retired from broadcasting A&M football and basketball following the 2017 season, but in 2019 was still calling the school's baseball games.

Now seventy-eight years old, Dan Lovett looks back fondly at his days as a member of the H/E/E SWC football radio network.

"I was a secondary guy, not a mainline (announcer), but it was a big deal (to do the games)," Lovett recalled in a 2019 interview. "Connie (Alexander) would get the big game each week, and if I was lucky, I'd get Rice against TCU," he laughed.

On September 26, 1970, Lovett drew a big-time assignment— the Texas A&M-Ohio State clash in Columbus, Ohio. The top-ranked Buckeyes featured such notables as legendary coach Woody Hayes, quarterback Rex Kern, and defensive back Jack Tatum. Some 85,000 partisan fans watched as the Buckeyes blew out the Aggies, 56-13, in what was one of A&M's worst all-time defeats.

Dan Lovett worked SWC games from 1966-70. (courtesy of Dan Lovett)

It was Lovett who dutifully reported the carnage to the folks back home in Texas.

"At one point during the broadcast of the game I said, 'looks like the Buckeyes can ask for the check at the half,' he recalled. "The McCann-Erickson executive who was in charge of the Humble Radio Network spoke with me when I returned from Columbus and said I should never use that expression again."

In an ironic twist, Lovett's grandson Kyle is named after Kyle Field, the home of the Aggies.

Lovett started with Humble in 1966 as a substitute color announcer, before moving up to full-time color and, finally, play-by-play. His last season with Humble-Enco was 1970.

It was pretty heady stuff for a twenty-five-year-old whose only experience doing football play-by-play had been calling Jefferson City High School Jays games out of the bed of a pickup truck in the end zone.

"I felt like it was a feather in my cap," Lovett said of his Humble days. "I certainly treasured that opportunity. Like I said, it was a big deal."

The South Dakota native grew up in Payette, Idaho, and arrived in Texas in 1964 as a news reporter for Gordon McLendon's KILT radio station in Houston. Shortly thereafter, he was dispatched to Vietnam to file news reports for the station.

In 1968, Lovett was named to the original "Eyewitness News" reporting team at Channel 13 (KTRK) in Houston. By then, he was doing sports reporting. Lovett initially did weekend sportscasts, but moved into the daily sports anchor slot after the death of longtime anchor Guy Savage. Ironically, Savage had served as a color announcer on some of the very first Humble games broadcast in 1935.

And, in addition to his TV duties and Humble network obligations, Lovett did radio play-by-play for the Houston Oilers for four years.

Lovett is the first to admit that while being a Humble announcer certainly carried a certain amount of prestige, the financial rewards were not as great.

"I think I made $75 a game for play-by-play and $45-50 for color, plus travel expenses that were very slim," he said with a chuckle. "On the road, I ate at the cheapest place I could find, unless I was doing a game in Dallas, where (friend-colleague) Verne Lundquist, who was doing Dallas Cowboys games on the radio, would take me out to some nice (dining) spots."

During this time, Lovett and fellow Houston-H/E/E broadcaster Gene Arnold became longtime friends.

Lovett had a few memorable experiences while doing play-by-play, many times with longtime color announcer Dave Smith.

"One year I was doing a Baylor-Rice game at Rice Stadium, and I had bad stomach pains, I mean really bad stomach pains," he said. "I had to leave the booth near the end of the first half, and Dave took over, but nothing was said to the audience about the different play-by-play voice."

After six years as Channel 13 sports anchor, Lovett left Houston for WABC-TV in New York, which was the start of an ABC Sports career that spanned three decades. During that time on the big stage, he covered Super Bowls, the World Series, and the Olympics.

After a decade in New York, Lovett's career took him to TV stations in San Francisco, Washington, D.C., and Ohio.

He retired from ABC in 2002 and resides with his wife in Houston.

Jack Dale Schmanke was to Texas Tech what Frank Fallon was to Baylor—a broadcasting icon.

After high school, Jack Dale (he legally changed his last name from Schmanke), a native of Alma, Kansas, attended radio trade school in Kansas City. After that were brief stops in Altus, Oklahoma, and Topeka, Kansas. When Dale arrived at radio station KFYO in Lubbock in 1952, little did he know it would mark the beginning of a remarkable fifty-year career in sportscasting—all the time based on the South Plains.

He originally broadcast football games on the Red Raider Network, but that was before Humble bought the rights to Tech football in 1953, leaving Dale in limbo, but only for a short time.

After writing a letter to Kern Tips, Dale was added to the Humble SWC announcing team in 1953 and continued in that role through the end of the network in 1977. After that, he continued to broadcast SWC and Tech games on the Mutual and then Host networks. He also did play-by-play for Texas Tech basketball for a half-century.

One of Dale's most memorable games was one he missed. In a 2002 interview with Jane Prince-Jones of KFYO radio in Lubbock, Dale related how, in the mid-1950s, he called a Friday night Lubbock High School game at Jones Stadium (Lubbock). He was scheduled to be the color man for Humble the following afternoon at a 1:30 p.m. game in Stillwater, Oklahoma.

"I had chartered an airplane for the next morning," Dale said. "I got up early Saturday morning and you couldn't see across the street in Lubbock, the fog was so bad. I hated to call that producer and tell him I wasn't going to be there. The play-by-play man did the pre-game, halftime, and play-by-play."

Needless to say, Dale never missed another H/E/E assignment.

The KFYO broadcasting crew of Don Opheim, Bob Nash, and Jack Dale works a Texas Tech basketball game. (courtesy of News/Talk 95.1 & 790 KFYO, Lubbock, Texas)

Dale retired from play-by-play duties in 2003, but continued to host a Lubbock sports-talk radio program until shortly before his death in 2011.

All told, he broadcast more than 1,300 men's basketball games and 47 college football seasons.

In a 1995 interview, Dale offered more pleasant memories.

"Those were enjoyable days," he said. "I didn't have Tech games every weekend, but I did get to go to a lot of different places. One year I went to South Bend to do the Rice-Notre Dame game. Another time, I went to West Point for the A&M-Army game."

Dale's distinctive voice and style were popular among listeners and complemented other top network announcers such as Kern Tips and Connie Alexander.

"(Whereas) I try to be quick and excited all the way through the game, Connie and Kern both used metaphors or rhyming phrases," he said. "My style is more to report things and be naturally excited."

His colleague Alexander said of Dale in 1969, "I had always heard Jack was a tremendous basketball announcer. But after hearing him in football, I can't imagine him being better at any other sport. He's clear and accurate, and always fully prepared."

Dale admitted that the H/E/E folks were very sensitive about its announcers showing absolutely no favoritism.

"People would send their (Humble) credit cards back to Houston if they were unhappy about a broadcast," he said.

One of his two sons, Steve, followed his father into sportscasting in Lubbock.

Tom Hedrick was the last former Exxon broadcaster to call a college football game: On November 10, 2018, Hedrick was behind the mic for the Baker University (Kansas)—Evangel University game. Then, on February 27, 2019, at age eighty-four, Hedrick broadcast

Tom Hedrick was the last former Exxon broadcaster to call a college football game when on November 10, 2018, he worked the Baker University (Kansas) – Evangel University contest. (courtesy of Baker University Athletics)

his final event—a basketball game between Baker and MidAmerica Nazarene University in Olathe, Kansas. He had served as the Voice of the Baker Wildcats (his alma mater) since 1988.

Thus concluded an impressive sixty-two-year career in the business. Hedrick is one of only two living sportscasters, as of this writing, who did play-by-play of Super Bowl I. The other is Jack Whitaker, now in his mid-90s.

One of Hedrick's most memorable games was played a decade before he arrived in the Exxon booth, although it involved an SWC team.

The date was September 18, 1965, and the Texas Tech Red Raiders were hosting the Kansas Jayhawks at Jones Stadium in Lubbock. Humble's top crew of Kern Tips and Alec Chesser were on the mic, as was young Tom Hedrick on the Kansas Jayhawks network.

Early in the fourth quarter, with torrential rain, high winds, and

Humble-Enco-Exxon utilized ads in various publications in marketing its radio network of SWC broadcasts throughout the Southwest. (courtesy of ExxonMobil)

tornadoes pummeling the area, the game was called with Tech leading 26-7.

Tips and Alec Chesser signed off the air as follows:

Unknown voice in the radio booth: *Mr. Tips, we better clear out because of the turbulent weather heading right toward us.*

Kern Tips: *This concludes our broadcast.*

In a 2019 interview about the game, Hedrick simply said, "I was scared to death."

The son of a Methodist minister and elementary school teacher, Hedrick worked at radio stations in Lawrence and Hutchinson (Kansas) and Kilgore, Texas, before taking over as the Voice of the Kansas Jayhawks in 1960. After that were stints at radio-TV stations in Lincoln (Nebraska), Kansas City, and Cincinnati.

He found his way to Dallas in 1973 as a sports anchor for KDFW (Channel 4) and quickly added Texas Rangers games, Exxon football, and Missouri Valley basketball to his busy work schedule.

"I did six or seven games a year in 1973-74—I was lucky, most guys had to wait ten years to get a job with the Exxon network," Hedrick said. "I had worked on nine Cotton Bowl games on CBS Radio with Connie Alexander (lead Exxon announcer,) and that opened some doors for me. I did mostly TCU, SMU or Baylor games."

During his career, he also called games for the Kansas City Chiefs, Cincinnati Reds, Dallas Cowboys, and Nebraska Cornhuskers. In addition, he worked three Super Bowls.

Just as impressive was how Hedrick taught university broadcasting classes for almost fifty years at KU and Baker. Along the way, he mentored eighty-two future broadcasters, including the likes of NFL-NBA and college basketball network announcer Kevin Harlan, CBS and cable TV news journalist Bill Kurtis, and longtime network sportscaster Gary Bender.

He and his wife reside in Lawrence.

EDDIE BARKER AND
THE REST IS HISTORY

If you lived in the Dallas-Fort Worth area in the 1950s/1960s, chances are good you remember hearing Eddie Barker on the radio and later seeing him on television on KRLD (later KDFW).

Barker was a short, red-headed gentleman who always had a friendly manner and pleasant look about him. But, according to associates, behind that look was a tough but fair-minded and well-loved old-time newsman.

Barker, who passed away in 2012 at age eighty-four, holds a chapter in the history of Humble radio broadcasting, as well as in the news reporting of the assassination of President John F. Kennedy in downtown Dallas.

But we'll get to all that.

Edmund Asa "Eddie" Barker, Jr. was born on August 18, 1927, in San Antonio.

While working at a

Eddie Barker is shown early in his broadcasting career. (courtesy of Susan Munguia)

radio station in his hometown in 1947, Barker was hired by Kern Tips and joined the Humble Southwest Conference announcing team.

The twenty-year-old, with booth partner Charlie Jordan, broadcast his first game that year in Norman, Oklahoma, as the Sooners hosted Texas A&M. Little did Barker know at the time that the Aggies would later play a cruel role in the fate of his career as a college sports announcer.

Two years into his Humble career, Barker joined the news staff of KRLD radio/TV (CBS affiliates in Dallas) and eventually became news director of both, earning national acclaim for his work.

Fast forward to October 6, 1962. Now into his sixteenth year of a rising Humble broadcasting career, it was all about to come to a sudden end.

Barker was providing play-by-play of the Texas Tech-Texas A&M game from College Station, with Glenn Brown serving as color announcer. The game was scoreless until the final minute, when Tech kicked a field goal. But then A&M returned the ensuing kickoff 100 yards with two seconds remaining for a 7-3 victory.

The following week, Tips unceremoniously fired Barker. And to this day, no one knows for sure why. Some blamed Tech boosters, others pointed fingers at the rabid Aggie fans.

Years later, longtime H/E/E announcer Jack Dale offered his take on the game and ill-fated aftermath.

"Neither team was worth a darn, and when they finally scored, Eddie got excited on the air," Dale said in an interview with the *Houston Chronicle*. "What is an announcer going to do? It was the most exciting play of the game. The next week, he was fired. Tech fans thought he was too partisan."

Barker offered a different perspective in his autobiography (*Eddie Barker's Notebook*), saying it was because he was behind the microphone for too many Aggie losses and fans didn't like what he said about the team.

Whatever the case, Barker wrote that it was a traumatic experience for him:

"The abrupt firing haunted me for many years. It crushed me. It was a humiliating experience. It was tough to explain to my wife and co-workers why I was so unceremoniously dumped after sixteen years. It wasn't the loss of the income that bothered me—I think I was making $125 a game—although when you're bringing up five kids, every little bit helps. It was the prestige of broadcasting Southwest Conference football that I loved most. But, besides the respect that came with being a Humble Network broadcaster, I enjoyed the games; I enjoyed the people; I enjoyed being a part of it all."

But what seemed to bother Barker more than anything else was how the termination was handled. Instead of facing Barker, Tips had fellow Humble announcer and KRLD co-worker Ves Box deliver the news. And Box delivered the bad news without giving a reason for the abrupt action.

Seeking answers, Barker called and sent letters to Tips, who reportedly never replied.

And what about Barker's significant role in history in reporting on the John F. Kennedy assassination?

On that fateful day—November 22, 1963—KRLD news director Eddie Barker was the first newsman to report the death of President Kennedy, making the announcement on a CBS feed to a national TV audience.

Barker was stationed at the Dallas Trade Mart, awaiting the president's arrival for a luncheon. But word spread quickly that something had gone terribly wrong. And while Barker was giving his live report on what little he knew, he was interrupted (on air) by a doctor friend who said the president was dead.

Following is the actual word-for-word account:

Barker: "The Texas School Book Depository, which is a building about eight floors in height…Yes? (Pause of seven seconds) as the doctor tells Barker the president is dead)….And who are you, sir?"

Doctor: "I don't want to be identified."

Barker: "We have just been told by a member of the staff at Parkland Hospital the president is dead. What is the governor's (John Connally's) condition?"

Doctor: "He's been shot in the chest."

Barker: "Do you have any report on that?"

Doctor: "No."

Barker: "Thank you, sir. This is the report of a doctor at Parkland Hospital, who was here for the luncheon. He says that the president is dead. We do not have a confirmation on this. We only pass it along as the word of a man who we take to be a good source at this time. The word we have is that President Kennedy is dead. This we do not know for a fact. . . . The word we have is from a doctor on the staff at Parkland Hospital who says that it is true. He was in tears when he told me just a moment ago."

Dallas broadcasting icon Eddie Barker signs copies of his autobiography, Eddie Barker's Notebook, which was published in 2006. (courtesy of Juan M. Garcia)

Barker became a Dallas broadcast icon in the 1960s and was the anchor for Channel 4's 6 p.m. and 10 p.m. news broadcasts. He left the station in 1972 and became executive vice president of VanCronkhite & Maloy Public Relations in Dallas. In 1973, he bought the company, which became Eddie Barker Associates, Inc.

After retirement, he returned to broadcasting, hosting a talk show on KPLT-AM in Paris, Texas, while also working weekends at KRLD.

BY MUTUAL AGREEMENT
WITH A HOST OF OTHERS

According to Chaucer (the great English poet)—who was no Dave Campbell (the great Texas sportswriter) by the way—all good things must come to an end.

Following the 1977 football season, Humble-Enco-Exxon and the Southwest Conference ended their storied relationship. For forty-four consecutive years (1934-1977) H/E/E had sponsored radio broadcasts of SWC football.

For the record, the last SWC game broadcast by the network was played at Kyle Field in College Station on December 3, 1977, when Texas A&M defeated the University of Houston, 27-7. Connie Alexander provided the play-by-play, with Dave Smith serving as color commentator.

"As far as I know, it was the longest continuous sponsorship in radio history," said Alec Chesser, Kern Tips's longtime color commentator, in a 1978 interview with the *Houston Post*. "It was the most unique business partnership in the country."

To be fair, there had been rumblings for years from some of the bigger SWC schools, who eyed national and team networks elsewhere that offered greater exposure and revenue.

As it turned out, the change was not without controversy.

In 1978, the Mutual Broadcasting System, a national organization founded in 1934, made a bid for the rights to broadcast SWC football.

Mutual was best known for such radio shows as *The Lone Ranger*, *The Adventures of Superman*, and *The Shadow*. It also broadcast news, talk shows, major league baseball, NFL football, and Notre Dame football.

In its proposal, Mutual offered the SWC $1.5 million over five years. The offer also expanded coverage of games to nine states (Texas-Arkansas-Arizona-Kansas-Louisiana-Mississippi-New Mexico-Oklahoma-Tennessee) across the 250-station Mutual Radio Network. In addition, several SWC games would be carried nationally in conjunction with Mutual's eleven Notre Dame games.

The only problem was the Texas State Network (TSN) was also interested in broadcasting the games. So TSN filed an injunction that allowed the company to offer its own visual presentation to the SWC powers-that-be. Like Mutual, TSN had a memorable history, having been founded in 1938 by Elliott Roosevelt, son of President Franklin Roosevelt.

TSN later withdrew the injunction after it was allowed to present its proposal. The TSN bid was $2.2 million and also offered coverage in several out-of-state markets, including New Mexico, Oklahoma, Arkansas, and Louisiana.

In addition to a renewal bid from Exxon, the SWC also considered putting an "in-house" radio network together.

Initially, several radio stations were not pleased with the original Mutual proposal, requiring a station to "select a package" of games, which did not include all their hometown team's games. In other words, stations would have to purchase all four of the network packages (an expensive proposition) to obtain all the games they wanted.

"In order to get the cream, you gotta buy the milk," said Mutual Executive Vice President Gary Worth. "What we're doing is preventing the cream from being skimmed. Otherwise, if we let the affiliate pick and choose, the weaker football schools will wind up being hurt."

Not surprisingly, that didn't set well with many affiliates across Texas.

In a series of articles in 1978, *The University Daily* (Texas Tech) reporter Chino Chapa did outstanding work in chronicling the changes in SWC radio. He elicited responses from all those involved, from radio network executives to station general managers to broadcasters to conference officials.

"I know some stations have bad sentiments toward it," said Jack Dale of KFYO in Lubbock, who was a longtime H/E/E broadcaster. "I don't think the Southwest Conference thought the releasing of Exxon would turn into a mess like this."

Added Bob Nash, also of KFYO: "We've been carrying the (Texas Tech) Raider games since 1931. That's two years before Exxon even began coverage. When Exxon took over, we said 'sure' just as long as we got to keep the Raider games. They agreed. Now this contract may not honor that agreement."

Nationally-known broadcaster Frank Glieber of KRLD in Dallas, who had also done a few Humble broadcasts in the late 1950s, had similar thoughts.

"We're not keen to this new proposal," he said. "We'd like to continue the (SMU) Mustang broadcasts, but we wouldn't be able to under this bid."

Under the old H/E/E agreement, if the traditional school broadcasting station carried only that school's game per week, the network entered the area market and bought time on other stations to get all SWC games within each geographic area.

When all was said and done, the SWC chose to go with Mutual, siding with more out-of-state coverage instead of the dollars offered by TSN.

Right away, longtime listeners of SWC football on the radio noticed some differences.

For one thing, more commercials, as in triple the number, going from 10 minutes of commercial interruption on Exxon to 32 on Mutual. Also, Mutual would not pay the station for air time, but would allow it to make its income by selling commercial time to local sponsors. Of the 32 commercial spots, 20 would belong to Mutual and 12 could be sold by the local station.

"That's what made our relationship with Exxon so remarkable," Chesser lamented to the *Post*. "Today there's a commercial during every timeout. We had one at the beginning, opening with the familiar 'Brought to you by your neighborhood Humble dealer,' another shortly before kickoff, one midway between each quarter, two at halftime, and another at signoff. In other words, no more than eight and a half or nine minutes of commercial time. We didn't overdo it."

Another notable change Mutual made was in its lineup of announcers. The network added familiar names such as Verne Lundquist, Brad Sham, Ray Gaskin, Bill Coates and Norm Hitzges of Dallas, Bill Mercer of Denton, Greg Lucas, Jim Nantz, and Steve Fallon, son of Frank Fallon.

To its credit, the network retained many of the veteran Exxon crew members, including play-by-play announcers such as Jack Dale, the elder Fallon, and Glenn Brown, along with color announcers Stan McKenzie, Dave South, Dave Smith, John Smith, and Ray Boyd.

But one marquee name was missing—Connie Alexander—who had been the top announcer for H/E/E for the preceding decade.

"We did talk some," Alexander recalled in an interview with the *Lubbock Avalanche-Journal,* a couple of years after the Exxon-SWC split. "And after our first discussion, I felt very optimistic that we could work things out to both our benefits. But it turned out that they (Mutual) weren't going to have a game-of-the-week format like Exxon. I expressed that I would only be interested in that since I had been Exxon's top play-by-play man for eleven years. But the game-of-the-week format wasn't in their plans."

Alexander, a longtime resident of Albuquerque, New Mexico, believed there was another factor working against him.

"I think Mutual wanted to use hometown people," he said." I really think that living outside the state was a factor. In fact, I was the only one to live outside the state when I worked for Exxon, too. I believe their (Mutual) thinking was the travel expense for me to and from games would be too costly."

Dave Smith, who handled color duties from 1951-77, much of the time alongside Alexander, stayed on with Mutual, at least for a little while.

"We learned some solid broadcast principles with Kern (Tips)," Smith recalled in a 1990 interview with Texas newspaper columnist Tumbleweed Smith. "The new boys didn't seem too interested in using those principles, so most of us quit. Kern told us not to worry if we didn't finish reading a commercial before play resumed because the entire broadcast of the game was a commercial."

As Mutual completed its first year of SWC broadcasts in 1978, there was already grumbling, with some school officials and radio station managers accusing the network of violating its contract.

The chief complaints were missed games and the excess commercials, including some that interrupted the play-by-play.

Frank Elliott, who chaired the Texas Tech Athletic Council at that time, told Chapa of *The University Daily* that 250 games had not been aired in the nineteen major Texas markets, adding that because of that, the conference had the right to break the contract.

"We didn't sign the contract with Mutual for the money," Elliott said. "We wanted exposure, and they haven't given us what they said they would."

Meanwhile, Mutual spokesman Ted Foster refuted that claim, saying, "I don't know where (Elliott) could have come up with such a number (of games missed). As far as I know, we have only missed ten games."

Foster also shifted the blame to the conference, saying league officials were tardy in notifying Mutual of changes in game dates, making logistics difficult.

As far as the radio stations, most of the smaller markets were happy with Mutual because they could afford to carry the games due to the packaging.

"Mutual has done everything Exxon didn't do," Ken Duke, general manager of KMRE in Dumas, told Chapa. "Exxon didn't help the smaller markets. We didn't have an SWC game broadcast by Exxon on this station for seventeen years. This year we aired twenty-eight games. The only reason the bigger markets aren't pleased is that they never have had to hustle to sell ads like us."

Bill Hooten, GM of KDSX in Sherman-Denison, agreed, telling the *The University Daily*, "This year's broadcasting was a success. We've been wanting Southwest Conference football for a long time, but Exxon didn't need us since they used the bigger stations. We're very happy we got this deal this year. Financially, we did very well."

But it was a different story for the bigger stations.

"We contracted with Mutual, but we have received quite a few complaints," said veteran KRLD (Dallas) sportscaster Frank Glieber. "The quality of the coverage was not as good as last year's (Exxon)."

Added Clive Griffen of KPRC in Houston: "The quality was terrible, their package system was poorly done, and we received a tremendous amount of complaints. I think they violated the contract with the Southwest Conference and should be reviewed."

Complaints or no complaints, the contract continued.

Unlike Humble, the Mutual-SWC agreement never made it close to forty-four years. In fact, the SWC did not renew with Mutual after the original five-year contract ended following the 1982 football season. Furthermore, the Mutual Broadcasting System ceased operations in 1999.

The SWC awarded its next radio contract to Host Communications of Lexington, Kentucky, in 1983.

More changes were underway. Under the Mutual format, a home announcer had been assigned to each SWC team. Host took the concept a step farther, as the competing teams each had an announcer in the booth, with the home team announcer handling play-by-play duties, and the visiting team announcer doing color. This made for some rather interesting exchanges, especially when the games were close, there were controversial calls, or if there was an exciting finish, as announcers did their best not to blatantly show their allegiance.

That concept never really caught on, but live cut-ins to other games did prove to be popular.

Longtime H/E/E broadcasters continuing on with Host after Mutual included Jack Dale, Dave South, Frank Fallon, and Glenn Brown. Among the "new" names were Ron Franklin, Craig Way, Chuck Cooperstein, and Craig Miller.

In the late 1980s and early 1990s, single-school networks came into being in the SWC and continue today. Most were operated by Host, Learfield Sports, and International Management Group (IMG College), all comprehensive marketing companies.

And each school has its own network with its own announcers.

For example, the Texas A&M Radio Network was born in 1988, thanks to the influence of then Aggie-coach Jackie Sherrill. According to Dave South, the Voice of the Aggies for thirty-two years, Sherrill set up a meeting with Jim Host, founder and CEO of Host Communications.

South related that story in a 2017 interview with Matt Simon of 12thMan.com:

"He got up there (for the meeting) and just flat out told Jim, "This is coming to an end. We're going to have our own network. Texas is going to have their own network…everybody else is going to have their own network.' And it's been that way ever since."

Added South: "It's better for the schools to have their own network. People tell me they turn down the TV and turn up the radio because they want to listen to a broadcast that supports the team they are supporting."

The A&M Network featured South doing play-by-play and former Aggie star Dave Elmendorf as analyst.

"The days of the old Exxon network, where Exxon made sure everybody got equal coverage, were gone," South said in his interview with Simon. "But it was the right way to go. Those smaller schools were riding the coattails of A&M and Texas."

In a 2017 interview with David Barron of the *Houston Chronicle*, South noted: "I work for the school. I don't work for Exxon. I work for Texas A&M as part of the broadcast that sells Aggies football. That's why I've been able to do this for forty-seven years. I understood what everyone wanted, and when I went to work for A&M, they wanted an Aggie broadcast."

In the same Barron column, Brad Sham, longtime radio voice of the Dallas Cowboys and who once worked for the Host SWC network, offered a more moderate view, saying he followed the standard set by colleague Verne Lundquist, who tried to "call an unbiased broadcast from a Dallas Cowboys perspective."

"I've tried to do that, too," Sham said. "There's nothing partisan about getting excited about a good football play. There's nothing wrong with showing excitement. The fans are excited, so why shouldn't we reflect that? There is a professional way to do so."

Bill Little, the now-retired longtime athletic communications guru at the University of Texas, recognized that while the Humble network benefited everyone, schools came to realize the true value of their own individual networks.

"You could present your message the way you wanted it, which is not what the conference network was set up to do," Little told Barron. "Besides, none of the coaches' wives liked Humble, because they thought the announcer was for the other team."

All of this was just a forerunner to major organizational change.

The SWC itself would dissolve in 1996, with Texas, Texas A&M, Baylor, and Texas Tech joining the Big 12 Conference, leaving SMU, Rice, Houston, and TCU to fend for themselves. Longtime league member Arkansas had bolted to the Southeastern Conference in 1992.

In 2011, along came the Longhorn Network, a regional sports television network that was a joint venture of the University of Texas, ESPN, and IMG College.

After a shaky and controversial launching, the Longhorn Network slowly began gaining viewers. However, the marketing and financial windfall of the project ruffled the feathers of the Longhorns' Big 12 opponents, hastening Texas A&M's departure from the league to join the Southeastern Conference in 2012.

In December of 2018, Learfield and IMG College merged into Learfield IMG College. Most of the old SWC schools use this company for not only broadcasting, but branding, licensing, publishing, sponsorship, and other marketing and promotional services. In other words, it's become big business—far more than the days of simple radio broadcasts.

And each school still has its own network and announcers.

In most cases, the current play-by-play announcers have stood the test of time.

Baylor's John Morris has been doing his school's games for 32 years, with analyst J. J. Joe alongside for 15 seasons; Brian Estridge has logged 21 seasons at TCU; Brian Jensen (19 years) and John Harris (36 years) are fixtures providing play-by-play and color, respectively, for Texas Tech; Craig Way at Texas and Rich Phillips at SMU are eighteen-year veterans at their respective schools; and Chuck Barrett has 11 years of experience at Arkansas.

John Harris, it should be noted, first began doing color for Texas Tech games back in the 1980s with Jack Dale on Host.

Among the 'newest' announcers in the fold are Kevin Eschenfelder, who's been at the University of Houston six years, and Andrew Monaco, who replaced longtime Aggie announcer Dave South in 2018.

While advancements in technology have undoubtedly improved many aspects of present-day college football radio broadcasts, all of these announcers owe a debt of gratitude to Kern Tips and the rest of the cast that came before them.

As longtime color announcer Dave Smith once reminisced of the H/E/E announcing experience:

"Arriving at a stadium early, wearing your Humble Jacket. Fans coming up to you and talking about the game. Those were the real awards and the real thrills."

The Texas Sports Hall of Fame in Waco features a special exhibit on the Broadcasters of the Southwest Conference. The display includes photographs, audio recordings and other memorabilia.

APPENDIX 1

(The following chapter is excerpted from *The Power and the Glory—The Story of Southwest Conference Football*, by Harold V. Ratliff, The Texas Tech Press, 1957. Literary Licensing LLC).

Man at the Mike

Kern Tips, as sports writer, broadcaster and telecaster, reported all the big moments of Southwest Conference football. No one ever was more closely associated with it or knew the intimate happenings of the game as Tips. His observations of football cover many angles:

A working observation of the Southwest Conference since its beginnings should condition anybody to the unfailing paradox of its football. Yet, I confess after all these years that wonder still grows at the indiscriminate manhandling of the pre-game forecast and the outrageous violations of the laws of probability.

Therein lies the great come-on of Southwest Conference football for its devotees year after year; more recent generations certainly are as awed by its unpredictability, as respectful of its practitioners, as proud of its national prominence as mine continues to be. I cannot fail to remark its year-by-year recurrence of the unexpected and unusual, the brilliant plays and players, the uncertainty of victory or defeat until the final whistle. This sort of gridiron treasure is a Confederate heritage.

Yesterday's greats were indeed great, but so are today's. Yesterday's thrills are unforgettable; so are today's. And tomorrow's will surely be as memorable. The spirit of derring-do is each new season's birthright.

Material change, of course, there has been—change in styles of play and tactics and strategy, in rules and regulations, in training method and uniform and equipment; in public interest and its by-product, larger stadia. And change, too, there has been in the balance of football power as graduation shook dynasties when their opponents could not shake them.

As a bird's eye-viewman, I am particularly aware of the changes in football's modern house with its new conveniences for spectators, press, radio, cameras and television.

As comparative newcomers to the field of football reporting, radio and TV have reason to be especially grateful for this evolution from wooden bleachers to spacious penthouses at the summit.

When radio was first invited to the party to provide organized coverage in 1934, it was a somewhat suspect guest. Even its more ardent pleaders had some misgivings that they might spawn a Frankenstein that would hypnotize the cash customer and pin him to his living room chair.

Suffice it to observe, however, that the fear soon vanished; today the Texas A&M-Texas game, for example, draws more spectators than either team drew during an entire season a few years ago.

But those who came to broadcast those early years can recall when our facilities could at best be called "temporary." Not infrequently, our microphones shared desk-space with sports writers' typewriters and telegraphers' bugs. Press-box conversation in the raw has never been for beaming to the radio receiver, and surely some of our earlier listeners were startled if not shocked by the salty side-bars from broadcasting's non-professionals within mike-shot of our equipment.

Today, our broadcasting booths are plush, soundproof chambers where the whisper seems the roar; this acoustical achievement has, however, ruled out the muncher of peanuts, the rustler of papers, the shuffler of feet, and especially, the more excitable who cannot restrain the spontaneous grunts, *ohs*, *ahs*, and *aws* that betray emotion.

How in the world, in this calm, and detached aerie could an announcer be so overwhelmed by it all that he spoke: "Good afternoon, Kern Tips; this is ladies and gentlemen speaking?" But he did.

Fortunately, however, reportorial accuracy is more frequently the hallmark of the announcer, thanks in large measure to our spotters. These generally are students, frequently athletes, injured or ineligible; they are drilled to keep their eyes open and their mouths shut. But after all, they're human, they're interested and they're biased. Spotters keep radio announcers out of a lot of trouble; they also furnish us some bad moments.

Some years ago, a track coach, off-duty in the fall, was assigned to us as a spotter; this cinder Svengali had been nursing along a sprinting Trilby, who was to make his fame. The football coach, needing speed in his backfield, dipped into the track ranks to bring up to the varsity this speed-merchant, though the boy was admittedly untutored in football.

Each week, the track coach from his vantage point in the broadcast booth, would eye his protégé on the bench and send up a silent prayer that he would not be called upon that day to risk limb on the gridiron. But one afternoon, the football coach fingered the dashman to do his bit; on his first play, sizzling into the line, he was smeared by the most vicious linebacker in the Conference.

Players huddled, trainers were called, our track coach blanched and all but fainted. When the sprint star emerged from the wreckage on the field, his head was swathed in a huge towel; the track coach was visibly relieved: "Thank heavens," he sighed into our microphones, "it was just his head."

Then there was the time we were assigned as our spotter an injured backfield star, his right leg sheathed in a cast. There was not enough room for him to stretch his unbending member forward, so he settled it in my lap; a little uncomfortable, I thought, for both of us. I had not realized that our casualty was also his team's star punter; each time either team punted that day, his right leg, cast and all, reflexed like a frog's leg in the frying pan. From my bruises on the thighs, I would say he had a seventy-yard punt average that afternoon in the broadcasting booth.

Through the more than two decades of Humble's broadcasts, certain policies have been evolved—the do's and don'ts that are observed in our narrations. Of paramount importance, perhaps, is the practice of sticking to the game and the things that bear upon it, sometimes to the exclusion of things that are exciting but extraneous.

There's one exception; injuries. We never comment on them. True, the removal of an injured lad from the lineup may bear upon the outcome. If you're at the game, you make your own appraisal; if you're listening miles away, you probably are not aware the boy has been hurt because we don't announce the fact. And there is one important part of our listening audience that has never questioned this policy—the boy's relatives and friends.

Suppose it is their boy who is carried off the field? Suppose it was yours? What could you do about it but suffer and pray until you could get the facts from somebody who *knew* the facts—hours later. Admittedly we don't have access to the facts, so we don't talk about injured football players. I'm sure we're right; letters from mothers and fathers of football players say we are.

Bottle throwing? Fights in the stands? Sideline accidents? These are exciting, but they don't affect the progress of the ball game; that's all we came to describe.

I shall never forget the day the stands collapsed at Ownby Stadium in Dallas while the Aggies were playing SMU. But nothing was said about it on our broadcast; it couldn't have helped—it could easily have been disastrous, by attracting throngs to the stadium, blocking avenues for ambulances and other emergency vehicles. I suppose, in looking back, your discretion wrestles briefly with your reportorial instinct; luckily that day, I believe judgment had the upper hand.

Cyclops, the television camera, has brought the ultimate electronic dimension to football reporting, for it lifts the stadium into living rooms miles away, removing the middleman for the viewer; the announcer ceases to be the listener's eye—he speaks only to the watcher's ear.

Now, all the great plays and players that you and I see at firsthand can be shared with and savored by millions; the appreciation of football as a sport and a spectacle is spread to new quarters, winning new friends and strengthening old ties. Interesting surveys show that women make up a good 40 per cent of TV football audience, giving lie to the classic stories that malign the lady at the football game. Football in the TV home is her genuine interest, or she'd look the other way.

Television's eye can now transport you to the field and let you share the intimacies of the huddle—show you the facial expressions that bespeak ecstasy and anger, desperation and disappointment—convince you that college football is still a game played mostly by minors boyishly eager to win, and not a band of padded and helmeted robots triggered in motion by a button in the quarterback's hand.

Of all the thrills of my business, the greatest is the opportunity to observe these Saturday Supermen in their relaxed moments when they're off-field, doing and saying the same things your son and mine do and say.

Unforgettably, there was the afternoon on the plane when one of our all-time great forward-passers was nursing a leg so banged-up he could hardly stand. Worried? Yes, he had a hangnail on the thumb of his throwing hand.

And the day one of the most rugged of our all-time tackles showed me a weather-beaten teddy bear from his childhood that he always laced to his trunks for good luck.

Or the evenings that one of our brainiest of all-time quarterbacks spent trying to master the intricacies of the yo-yo—and never did.

Football broadcasters and telecasters are lucky guys; and when they work in the Southwest Conference, they are thriced-blessed with fine coaches, outstanding officiating and terrific football players. Truly, ours is a privileged profession.

APPENDIX 2

Announcer's Script
Arkansas Vs. SMU (1945)
(courtesy of Ronnie Perry)

franke · Wilkinson · Schwetz · inc.

RADIO CONTINUITY

DICK BUSH   Page 1

Station________________________ Date Nov. 17, 1945 ________ Time 2:15 P.M.

Program____ S. M. U. vs Arkansas U. ________ Client________ Humble Oil & Ref. Co.

KRLD - Dallas
KTRH - Houston

OPEN

Good afternoon, ladies and gentlemen. This is Dick Bush
speaking to you from Ownby Stadium in Dallas, Texas, to open
Humble Oil and Refining Company's broadcast of the football game between Southern Methodist University and Arkansas University, brought
to you as one more service under the Humble sign. Charlie Jordon will
give the play-by-play description of this afternoon's game and will
take over at the kick-off.

franke · Wilkinson · Schiwetz · inc.
RADIO CONTINUITY   DICK BUSH   Page___5___

Station_________________________Date____Nov. 17,1945________Time__2:15 P.M.______

Program___S.M.U.___vs Arkansas U.__________Client__Humble Oil & Ref. Co.__________

MIDDLE OF HALF-TIME

And now let's take a look at next week's Southwest Conference
schedule - that's for Saturday, November 24th.   Arkansas is the only
Conference team playing outside competition; they take on the University of Tulsa at Tulsa - duplicating Baylor's schedule for this
afternoon. The University of Texas and Texas A. & M. rest next
Saturday preparatory to their traditional game at College Station
on Thursday, November 29th. At Waco - this is on next Saturday -
the Baylor Bears play S.M.U.'s Mustangs, while Rice and T.C.U.
renew their Conference rivalry at Fort Worth. See one of these
games if you can; if you can't, tune in on a Humble broadcast.
Saturday afternoon at this season of the year belongs to football -
let Humble take you to the games or bring the games to you.

franke · Wilkinson · Schiwetz · inc.
RADIO CONTINUITY   DICK BUSH   Page___6___

Station_________________________Date____Nov. 17,1945________Time__2:15 P.M.______

Program___S.M.U.___vs Arkansas U.__________Client____Humble Oil & Ref. Co.________

BEFORE SECOND HALF KICK-OFF

The teams are returning to the field for the second half,
and Charlie Jordon is ready to take over for the kick-off. Just let
me remind you, first, that this game between Southern Methodist University
and Arkansas University is brought to you from Ownby Stadium in Dallas,
Texas, by Humble Oil and Refining Company as one more service to Texas
motorists under the Humble sign. Now, Charlie Jordon and the second
half.

franke · Wilkinson · Schwetz · inc.

RADIO CONTINUITY

DICK BUSH

Page 8

Station___________________ Date Nov. 17,1945 ___________ Time 2:15 P.M.___________

Program S.M.U. vs Arkansas U.___________ Client Humble Oil & Ref.Co.___________

CLOSE

And now, the Humble Company, its employees, service stations
and dealers, bid you all good afternoon.

APPENDIX 3

Timeline of Memorable Moments

FALL 1912:

The University of Minnesota's experimental radio station, 9X1-WLB, broadcasts a Minnesota football game using a spark transmitter and regular telegraphic signals.

NOVEMBER 27, 1919:

Three Texas A&M cadets utilize a telegraph machine to "broadcast" the Texas-Texas A&M game from College Station.

OCTOBER 8, 1921:

First live radio broadcast of a college football game—by KDKA—West Virginia vs. Pittsburgh.

NOVEMBER 26, 1925:

First actual radio broadcast of a football game in Texas, from College Station. Play-by-play of the Texas-Texas A&M game was handled by General Ike Ashburn, former A&M commandant.

OCTOBER 27, 1934:

First Southwest Conference radio broadcast sponsored by Humble Oil and Duncan Coffee—Texas at Rice. Houston sportswriter Lloyd Gregory did the play-by-play.

SEPTEMBER 21, 1935:

First SWC radio broadcast by Kern Tips—Rice at St. Mary's (San Antonio).

SEPTEMBER 30, 1944:

Color announcer Alec Chesser broadcasts his first Humble game (Texas A&M vs. Texas Tech) with play-by-play announcer Bill Michaels in San Antonio.

DECEMBER 1, 1945:

The first network telecast of a college football game (Army-Navy) is carried by NBC in four cities.

OCTOBER 11, 1947:

Future radio legend Gordon McLendon serves as color announcer with Bill Michaels on Humble broadcast of Texas A&M-LSU game.

NOVEMBER 13, 1948:

First live telecast in-state of an SWC game (Texas at TCU) on WBAP and sponsored by Humble.

JANUARY 12, 1951:

NCAA votes to restrict football telecasting—thereby limiting the number of games any team may be shown and imposing a total blackout on several days—to protect gate receipts.

SEPTEMBER 19, 1953:

First Humble network broadcast of a Texas Tech game: West Texas State College at Texas Tech, with Eddie Barker on play-by-play and Jack Dale doing color.

1953:

For the first time in NCAA college football history, television profits exceed radio profits.

1955:

After NCAA relaxes telecasting restrictions, Humble begins sponsoring regional telecasts.

OCTOBER 20, 1956:

Texas A&M defeats No. 4 TCU, 7-6, in what was known as "the Hurricane Game." Rain and hail halted the game in the second quarter in College Station. "More than 150 planes at Easterwood Airport were overturned, and the playing field became 100 yards of pig slop," according to *Pride in Aggieland.*

OCTOBER 11, 1958:

Twenty-four-year-old Frank Glieber provides color commentary with play-by-play announcer Dave Russell at the Baylor-Duke game. Glieber would later be a nationally recognized TV broadcaster for CBS, most notably for pro football and golf.

1960:

Humble broadcasts Texas high school football playoff games for the first time.

1961:

The Humble network is now referred to as the Enco network.

SEPTEMBER 22, 1962:

First Humble SWC broadcast by Connie Alexander (Jack Dale color)—West Texas State at Texas Tech.

OCTOBER 6, 1962:

Last Humble SWC broadcast by Eddie Barker—Texas Tech at Texas A&M. Barker was fired by Kern Tips for reportedly showing favoritism after criticism from listeners.

SEPTEMBER 18, 1965:

The Kansas-Texas Tech game at Jones Stadium in Lubbock ends early in the fourth quarter after torrential rain, high winds, and tornadoes pummel the area; Humble announcers Kern Tips and Alec Chesser sign off the air with Tech leading 26-7. Calling the game on the Kansas Jayhawks network is Tom Hedrick, who will announce games on the Exxon network in the mid-1970s.

DECEMBER 17, 1966:

Last Humble broadcast by Kern Tips—Bluebonnet Bowl at Rice Stadium (Ole Miss vs. Texas).

AUGUST 3, 1967:

Kern Tips dies of cancer in Houston at the age of sixty-two.

DECEMBER 6, 1969:

The Big Shootout between number-one-ranked Texas and number-two Arkansas is played in Fayetteville, Arkansas, with President Richard Nixon in attendance. Texas wins, 15-14, on a late score; Humble announcers Connie Alexander and Stan McKenzie describe the action.

OCTOBER 30, 1971:

TCU Coach Jim Pittman collapses and dies of a heart attack on the sidelines during the TCU-Baylor game at Baylor Stadium. Because of strict network guidelines, radio announcers Jim Wiggins and Gene Arnold are not allowed to mention the event on air.

1973:

The Enco network is now referred to as the Exxon network.

OCTOBER 26, 1974:

In a game played at Legion Field in Birmingham, Alabama, TCU running back Kent Waldrep suffers a paralyzing injury. Again, due to network guidelines, Exxon radio announcers Frank Fallon and Gene Arnold are not allowed to discuss the injury.

FALL 1976:

The University of Houston joins the SWC; Cougar Radio network replaced by the Exxon network.

DECEMBER 3, 1977:

In the last SWC radio broadcast sponsored by Exxon, Texas A&M beats Houston, 27-7, at Kyle Field. Connie Alexander handles the play-by-play, with Dave Smith providing color.

MAY 6, 1978:

The SWC ends a forty-four-year relationship with Humble-Exxon by signing a five-year agreement for $1.5 million with Mutual Radio.

APPENDIX 4

Roster of Announcers

Following is a list of known announcers who broadcast at least one game on the Humble/Enco/Exxon radio network, with years active on the network, and city in which they were based at the time. (* = not consecutive years):

Connie Alexander	(1962-77)	Albuquerque, New Mexico
Gene Arnold	(1968-77)	Houston
Eddie Barker	(1947-62)	San Antonio-Dallas
Bob Barry	(1974-77)	Fort Worth
Buddy Bostick	(1939-50*)	Waco
Ray Boyd	(1965-77)	Lubbock
Ves Box	(1938-67)	Dallas
Conrad Brady	(1939)	Dallas
Glenn Brown	(1951-77*)	Austin
Dick Bush	(1945)	
Coit Butler	(1952-57)	San Antonio
Dave Byrn	(1938, 1942-43)	
Gene Cagle	(1937-38)	Fort Worth-McAllen
Tee Casper	(1940-41)	Fort Worth
Hal Chesnut	(1977)	Fort Worth
Alec Chesser	(1944-67)	San Antonio-Houston
Ray Cullin	(1955)	Lubbock-Amarillo
Joe Cullinane	(1953-54)	Houston
Bob Dahlgren	(1977)	Dallas-Fort Worth
Jack Dale	(1953-77)	Lubbock
Ed Dittert	(1948)	Beaumont

Jerry Doggett	(1944-56)	Dallas
Eddie Dunn	(1938-39)	Dallas-Chicago
Mike Edmonds	(1977)	Houston
Gene Elston	(1976-77)	Houston
Frank Fallon	(1970-77)	Waco
John Ferguson	(1951-54)	Baton Rouge, Louisiana
Jack Flaherty	(1938)	
Pat Flaherty	(1938-43*)	Houston-San Antonio
Eddie Gallaher	(1937)	Tulsa
Francis Gilbert	(1945)	
Frank Glieber	(1958-59)	Dallas
Lloyd Gregory	(1934)	Houston
Harry Grier	(1936)	Houston
George Harding	(1944)	Dallas
Gene Heard	(1947)	
Tom Hedrick	(1973-74)	Dallas
Bill Hightower	(1936-37)	Dallas-Fort Worth
Bob Hill	(1968-72)	
Eddie Hill	(1951-77)	Dallas
Tom Holbrook	(1945)	
Bob Holton	(1943)	Dallas
Tom Jacobs	(1936-43*)	Houston-Little Rock
Charlie Jordan	(1941-52)	Dallas-Fort Worth
Bill Karn	(1940-41)	Pampa-Cincinnati-Dallas
Fred Kincaid	(1941-49*)	Paris
Fritz Kuler	(1945)	Dallas
Cy Leland	(1935-41)	Fort Worth
Paul Lindsey	(1935)	
Dan Lovett	(1966-70)	Houston
Dick Lyons	(1944, 46)	
Carl Mann	(1950, 56)	Houston
Stan McKenzie	(1955-77)	Seguin
Gordon McLendon	(1947)	Dallas

Bill Michaels	(1941-53)	San Antonio
Mike Mistovich	(1954-72*)	Bryan
Jack Mitchell	(1937-38)	
Ted Nabors	(1943)	Houston
Fred Nahas	(1941-45*)	Houston
Bob Nash	(1967-71)	Lubbock
Bill Newkirk	(1942-49*)	Houston
Tim Osborne	(1973-74)	Houston
Fort Pearson	(1934-36*)	Chicago
John Phelan	(1956-57)	El Paso
Dan Riss	(1939-42)	Dallas-Cincinnati
Dave Russell	(1940-61*)	Beaumont-Dallas
Byrum Saam	(1935)	Fort Worth
Guy Savage	(1935)	Houston
Bud Sherman	(1938-39)	Fort Worth
Francis Siebert	(1945)	
Dave Smith	(1951-77)	Austin
John Smith	(1957-77)	Memphis, Tennessee
Dave South	(1970-77)	Waco
Ron Stone	(1971-73)	Houston
Rudy Tellez	(1957)	El Paso
Hal Thompson	(1937-50*)	Dallas-Fort Worth
Kern Tips	(1935-66)	Houston
Bob Tongo	(1938)	
Bob Walker	(1950-61)	Waco-Wichita Falls
Bill Ware	(1936)	Dallas
Harfield Weeden	(1938-43*)	Dallas-Austin-Houston
Jim Wiggins	(1949-77)	San Antonio
Steve Wilhelm	(1935)	
Gene Wyatt	(1935-38)	
Dave Young	(1939-41)	

NO. 1 PLAY-BY-PLAY
1935-1966 Kern Tips
1967-77   Connie Alexander

NO. 2 PLAY-BY-PLAY
1935-41   Cy Leland
1942-63   Ves Box
1964-66   Connie Alexander

NO. 1 COLOR
1946-66   Alec Chesser
1967-77   Stan McKenzie/Dave Smith

MOST YEARS WORKED
33   Kern Tips   (1935-66)
30   Ves Box   (1938-67)
29   Jim Wiggins   (1949-77)
27   Eddie Hill   (1951-77)
27   Dave Smith   (1951-77)
26   Glenn Brown   (1951-77)*
25   Jack Dale   (1953-77)
24   Alec Chesser   (1944-67)
23   Stan McKenzie (1955-77)
21   John Smith   (1957-77)
20   Dave Russell   (1940-61)*

APPENDIX 5

Announcers Year-by-Year

Following is a list of Humble/Enco/Exxon radio network announcers, listed by year. Play-by-play announcers are listed in the first grouping, followed by color announcers (+). In some cases, announcers are listed twice in the same year as they handled play-by-play or color announcing duties at different games.

1934

Lloyd Gregory
Fort Pearson

1935

Kern Tips
Byrum Saam
Gene Wyatt
Cy Leland
+Cy Leland
+Guy Savage
+Paul Lindsey
+Byrum Saam
+Gene Wyatt
+Steve Wilhelm

1936

Kern Tips
Bill Ware
Cy Leland
Gene Wyatt
Fort Pearson
+Bill Hightower
+Tom Jacobs
+Gene Wyatt
+Harry Grier
+Cy Leland
+Bill Ware

1937

Kern Tips
Cy Leland
Gene Cagle
Hal Thompson
Eddie Gallaher
Tom Jacobs
+Gene Wyatt
+Bill Hightower
+Tom Jacobs
+Jack Mitchell
+Eddie Gallaher
+Hal Thompson

1938
Kern Tips
Cy Leland
Ves Box
Hal Thompson
Eddie Dunn
+Jack Flaherty
+Eddie Dunn
+Harfield Weedin
+Bob Tongo
+Ves Box
+Dave Byrn
+Pat Flaherty
+Hal Thompson
+Bud Sherman
+Gene Cagle
+Jack Mitchell
+Gene Wyatt
+Cy Leland

1939
Kern Tips
Cy Leland
Eddie Dunn
Hal Thompson
+Harfield Weedin
+Eddie Dunn
+Hal Thompson
+Buddy Bostick
+Conrad Brady
+Bud Sherman
+Dan Riss
+Dave Young

1940
Kern Tips
Cy Leland
Hal Thompson
Ves Box
Dave Young
Dan Riss
+Pat Flaherty
+Buddy Bostick
+Tom Jacobs
+Dave Russell
+Tee Casper
+Dave Young
+Ves Box
+Hal Thompson
+Cy Leland
+Bill Karn

1941
Kern Tips
Cy Leland
Dave Young
Hal Thompson
Ves Box
Dan Riss
Charlie Jordan
Bill Michaels
+Tee Casper
+Dave Russell
+Bill Karn
+Hal Thompson
+Fred Kinkaid
+Fred Nahas
+Jerry Doggett
+Cy Leland

1942
Kern Tips
Charlie Jordan
Dan Riss
Ves Box
Bill Michaels
Dave Russell
+Dave Byrn
+Dave Russell
+Bill Newkirk
+Buddy Bostick
+Harfield Weedin
+Tom Jacobs
+Bill Michaels
+Charlie Jordan

1943
Kern Tips
Ves Box
Bill Michaels
Charlie Jordan
Dave Russell
+Dave Russell
+Tom Jacobs
+Ted Nabors
+Buddy Bostick
+Harfield Weedin
+Bob Holton
+Dave Byrn
+Pat Flaherty
+Charlie Jordan
+Bill Michaels
+Ves Box

1944

Kern Tips
Charlie Jordan
Bill Michaels
Ves Box
Dave Russell
+Dave Russell
+Fred Kincaid
+Alec Chesser
+Fred Nahas
+Charlie Jordan
+Bill Michaels
+Jerry Doggett
+Dick Lyons
+George Harding
+Ves Box

1945

Kern Tips
Charlie Jordan
Ves Box
Bill Michaels
Dave Russell
+Alec Chesser
+Fritz Kuler
+Fred Kincaid
+Dick Bush
+Fred Nahas
+Tom Holbrook
+Dave Russell
+Jerry Doggett
+Francis Siebert
+Francis Gilbert
+Bill Michaels
+Charlie Jordan

1946

Kern Tips
Bill Michaels
Ves Box
Charlie Jordan
Hal Thompson
+Alec Chesser
+Bill Hightower
+Fred Kincaid
+Jerry Doggett
+Dick Lyons
+Dave Russell
+Bill Michaels

1947

Kern Tips
Ves Box
Fred Kincaid
Charlie Jordan
Jerry Doggett
Bill Michaels
+Alec Chesser
+Bill Newkirk
+Eddie Barker
+Fred Kincaid
+Gordon McLendon
+Jerry Doggett
+Gene Heard

1948

Kern Tips
Charlie Jordan
Bill Michaels
Ves Box
Eddie Barker
Jerry Doggett
Ed Dittert
+Alec Chesser
+Jerry Doggett
+Fred Kincaid
+Buddy Bostick
+Bill Newkirk
+Hal Thompson
+Eddie Barker

1949

Kern Tips
Charlie Jordan
Ves Box
Bill Michaels
Eddie Barker
Dave Russell
+Alec Chesser
+Jerry Doggett
+Fred Kincaid
+Buddy Bostick
+Hal Thompson
+Bill Newkirk
+Jim Wiggins
+Eddie Barker

1950

Kern Tips
Ves Box
Jerry Doggett
Charlie Jordan
Bill Michaels
Eddie Barker
Dave Russell
+Alec Chesser
+Buddy Bostick
+Hal Thompson
+Jim Wiggins
+Jerry Doggett
+Dave Russell
+Eddie Barker
+Bob Walker
+Carl Mann

1951

Kern Tips
Ves Box
John Ferguson
Charlie Jordan
Dave Russell
Bill Michaels
+Alec Chesser
+Glenn Brown
+Bob Walker
+Dave Smith
+Eddie Hill
+Dave Russell
+John Ferguson
+Eddie Barker
+Jerry Doggett
+Jim Wiggins

1952

Kern Tips
John Ferguson
Charlie Jordan
Ves Box
Bob Walker
Bill Michaels
+Alec Chesser
+Dave Russell
+Eddie Barker
+Bob Walker
+Dave Smith
+Jerry Doggett
+Coit Butler
+Jim Wiggins
+John Ferguson

1953

Kern Tips
Eddie Barker
John Ferguson
Ves Box
Dave Russell
Bob Walker
Bill Michaels
+Jack Dale
+Dave Smith
+Coit Butler
+Alec Chesser
+Joe Cullinane
+Eddie Hill
+Bob Walker
+Eddie Barker
+Jerry Doggett
+Jim Wiggins

1954

Kern Tips
Dave Russell
Bob Walker
John Ferguson
Ves Box
Jerry Doggett
Eddie Barker
+Eddie Barker
+Coit Butler
+Jerry Doggett
+Eddie Hill
+Dave Smith
+Jack Dale
+Joe Cullinane
+Jim Wiggins
+Mike Mistovich
+Dave Russell
+Bob Walker

1955

Kern Tips
Ves Box
Dave Russell
Bob Walker
Stan McKenzie
Ray Cullin
Eddie Barker
Jerry Doggett
+Eddie Barker
+Alec Chesser
+Stan McKenzie
+Dave Smith
+Eddie Hill
+Mike Mistovich
+Jack Dale
+Coit Butler
+Jim Wiggins
+Jerry Doggett
+Ray Cullin

1956

Kern Tips
Ves Box
John Phelan
Dave Russell
Eddie Barker
Bob Walker
Eddie Hill
Jerry Doggett
Dave Russell
+Alec Chesser
+Jim Wiggins
+Mike Mistovich
+Stan McKenzie
+Carl Mann
+Dave Smith
+Jack Dale
+Eddie Hill
+Coit Butler
+Eddie Barker
+Jerry Doggett

1957

Kern Tips
Eddie Hill
Dave Russell
Eddie Barker
Bob Walker
Ves Box
Jack Dale
Jim Wiggins
John Phelan
+Alec Chesser
+Dave Smith
+John Smith
+Jim Wiggins
+Mike Mistovich
+Stan McKenzie
+Coit Butler
+Eddie Barker
+Jack Dale
+Rudy Tellez
+Eddie Hill

1958

Kern Tips
Ves Box
Dave Russell
Bob Walker
Eddie Barker
Eddie Hill
Jim Wiggins
+Jack Dale
+Alec Chesser
+Jim Wiggins
+John Smith
+Dave Smith
+Glenn Brown
+Stan McKenzie
+Jim Wiggins
+Frank Glieber
+Eddie Hill

1959

Kern Tips
Bob Walker
Dave Russell
Ves Box
Eddie Barker
Eddie Hill
Jim Wiggins
+Eddie Hill
+Jim Wiggins
+Alec Chesser
+Stan McKenzie
+Frank Glieber
+John Smith
+Jack Dale
+Glenn Brown
+Dave Smith

1960

Kern Tips
Ves Box
Bob Walker
Eddie Barker
Eddie Hill
Dave Russell
+Jim Wiggins
+Alec Chesser
+John Smith
+Stan Mckenzie
+Dave Smith
+Glenn Brown
+Jack Dale
+Eddie Hill

1961

Kern Tips
Ves Box
Jim Wiggins
Eddie Barker
Bob Walker
Eddie Hill
Dave Russell
+Alex Chesser
+Mike Mistovich
+Dave Smith
+John Smith
+Glenn Brown
+Jack Dale
+Stan McKenzie
+Jim Wiggins
+Eddie Hill

1962

Kern Tips
Eddie Hill
Ves Box
Eddie Barker
Jim Wiggins
Connie Alexander
Glenn Brown
+Alec Chesser
+Dave Smith
+Glenn Brown
+Stan McKenzie
+John Smith
+Jack Dale
+Jim Wiggins
+Mike Mistovich

1963

Kern Tips
Eddie Hill
Connie Alexander
Ves Box
Glenn Brown
Jim Wiggins
+Alec Chesser
+Stan McKenzie
+Jim Wiggins
+John Smith
+Jack Dale
+Eddie Hill
+Mike Mistovich
+Dave Smith

1964

Kern Tips
Connie Alexander
Ves Box
Eddie Hill
Jack Dale
Jim Wiggins
Alec Chesser
+Glenn Brown
+Jack Dale
+John Smith
+Stan McKenzie

1965

Kern Tips
Eddie Hill
Jack Dale
Jim Wiggins
Ves Box
Connie Alexander
Glenn Brown
+Alec Chesser
+John Smith
+Ray Boyd
+Mike Mistovich
+ Stan McKenzie
+Dave Smith
+Glenn Brown
+Jack Dale

1966

Kern Tips
Eddie Hill
Jim Wiggins
Jack Dale
Connie Alexander
Glenn Brown
+Alec Chesser
+Ray Boyd
+John Smith
+Stan McKenzie
+Dave Smith
+Dan Lovett
+Mike Mistovich

1967

Connie Alexander
Jim Wiggins
Eddie Hill
Jack Dale
Glenn Brown
John Smith
Dan Lovett
Ves Box
+Dave Smith
+Mike Mistovich
+Bob Nash
+Stan McKenzie
+Dan Lovett
+Alec Chesser
+John Smith

1968

Connie Alexander
Jack Dale
Dan Lovett
Eddie Hill
John Smith
Jim Wiggins
Glenn Brown
+Bob Nash
+Dan Lovett
+Gene Arnold
+Stan McKenzie
+Dave Smith
+Mike Mistovich
+Bob Hill
+Ray Boyd
+Jim Wiggins

1969

Connie Alexander
Eddie Hill
Jack Dale
Jim Wiggins
John Smith
Dan Lovett
+Gene Arnold
+Dave Smith
+Mike Mistovich
+Stan McKenzie
+Ray Boyd
+Bob Hill
+Bob Nash

1970

Connie Alexander
Glenn Brown
Eddie Hill
John Smith
Dan Lovett
Jack Dale
John Smith
+Stan McKenzie
+Bob Hill
+Dave Smith
+Gene Arnold
+Ray Boyd

1971

Connie Alexander
Jim Wiggins
Eddie Hill
Frank Fallon
Jack Dale
Glenn Brown
John Smith
+Mike Mistovich
+Ray Boyd
+Stan McKenzie
+Bob Hill
+Bob Nash
+Gene Arnold
+Dave Smith
+Ron Stone
+John Smith
+Dave South

1972

Connie Alexander
John Smith
Frank Fallon
Eddie Hill
Jack Dale
Jim Wiggins
Glenn Brown
+Gene Arnold
+Dave Smith
+Mike Mistovich
+Ron Stone
+Stan McKenzie
+Bob Hill
+Ray Boyd

1973

Connie Alexander
Jack Dale
Eddie Hill
Frank Fallon
Jim Wiggins
Glenn Brown
Tom Hedrick
+Dave Smith
+John Smith
+Stan McKenzie
+Gene Arnold
+Ray Boyd
+Tim Osborne
+Ron Stone

1974

Connie Alexander
Jack Dale
Tom Hedrick
Frank Fallon
Eddie Hill
Jim Wiggins
Glenn Brown
+John Smith
+Tim Osborne
+Stan McKenzie
+Dave Smith
+Bob Barry
+Ray Boyd
+Gene Arnold

1975

Connie Alexander
Frank Fallon
Eddie Hill
Glenn Brown
Jack Dale
Jim Wiggins
+John Smith
+Gene Arnold
+Dave Smith
+Stan McKenzie
+Ray Boyd
+Bob Barry

1976

Connie Alexander
Jack Dale
Gene Elston
Frank Fallon
Eddie Hill
Glenn Brown
Jim Wiggins
+John Smith
+Gene Arnold
+Stan McKenzie
+Bob Barry
+Ray Boyd
+Dave South
+Dave Smith

1977

Connie Alexander
John Smith
Eddie Hill
Jim Wiggins
Gene Elston
Frank Fallon
Jack Dale
Glenn Brown
+Dave South
+Stan McKenzie
+Ron Stone
+Ray Boyd
+Bob Dahlgren
+Mike Edmonds
+Bob Barry
+Hal Chesnut
+John Smith
+Gene Arnold
+Dave Smith

APPENDIX 6

Week-by-Week Game Assignments

Following are weekly game-by-game assignments for the Humble/ Enco/Exxon announcing teams. Information was compiled from the archives of more than one hundred Texas newspapers, with some game dates/information unavailable. Play-by-play announcer is listed first, followed by /color announcer.

1934

- **OCTOBER 27, 1934**
  Texas-Rice Lloyd Gregory

- **NOVEMBER 10, 1934**
  Rice-Arkansas

1935

- **SEPTEMBER 21, 1935**
  Rice-St. Mary's Kern Tips (Tips's first game)

- **SEPTEMBER 28, 1935**
  LSU-Rice Kern Tips/Byrum Saam

- **OCTOBER 12, 1935**
  SMU-Washington Kern Tips/Cy Leland (St. Louis)
  Creighton-Rice Byrum Saam/Guy Savage
  Arkansas-Baylor Gene Wyatt/Paul Lindsey

- **OCTOBER 19, 1935**
  Rice-SMU Kern Tips/Cy Leland
  Texas A&M-TCU Byrum Saam/Guy Savage
  Centenary-Texas Gene Wyatt

- **OCTOBER 26, 1935**
Rice-Texas Byrum Saam/Guy Savage
TCU-Centenary
SMU-Hardin-Simmons
Baylor-Texas A&M Kern Tips/Cy Leland
College of the Ozarks-Arkansas

- **NOVEMBER 2, 1935**
Texas-SMU Kern Tips/Cy Leland
TCU-Baylor Byrum Saam/Guy Savage
Texas A&M-Arkansas Gene Wyatt

- **NOVEMBER 9, 1935**
Arkansas-Rice Gene Wyatt
Texas-Baylor Byrum Saam/Guy Savage

- **NOVEMBER 16, 1935**
SMU-Arkansas Gene Wyatt/Tom Jacobs
TCU-Texas Byrum Saam/Steve Wilhelm

- **NOVEMBER 22, 1935**
Arkansas-Texas Byrum Saam/Gene Wyatt

- **NOVEMBER 23, 1935**
Rice-TCU Cy Leland/Kern Tips
Baylor-SMU Byrum Saam/Gene Wyatt

- **NOVEMBER 30, 1935**
SMU-TCU Kern Tips-NBC Byrum Saam-Columbia

- **DECEMBER 7, 1935**
SMU-Texas A&M Kern Tips/Cy Leland

1936

- **SEPTEMBER 26, 1936**

  Rice-LSU Kern Tips/Cy Leland

- **OCTOBER 3, 1936**

  Arkansas-TCU Kern Tips/Cy Leland

  LSU-Texas Bill Ware/Harry Grier

  Centenary-Baylor Gene Wyatt/Tom Jacobs

- **OCTOBER 10, 1936**

  Texas A&M-Rice Kern Tips/Cy Leland

  SMU-Fordham

  Baylor-Arkansas

- **OCTOBER 17, 1936**

  TCU-Texas A&M Fort Pearson/Gene Wyatt

  Baylor-Texas Bill Ware/Tom Jacobs

  Vanderbilt-SMU Kern Tips/Cy Leland

- **OCTOBER 24, 1936**

  Texas-Rice Kern Tips/Cy Leland

  Texas A&M-Baylor Bill Ware/Gene Wyatt

- **OCTOBER 31, 1936**

  Arkansas-Texas A&M Kern Tips/Bill Hightower

  SMU-Texas Bill Ware/Tom Jacobs

  Baylor-TCU Gene Wyatt/Cy Leland

- **NOVEMBER 7, 1936**

  Rice-Arkansas Bill Ware/Gene Wyatt

  Texas-TCU Cy Leland/Tom Jacobs

  Texas A&M-SMU Kern Tips/Bill Hightower

- **NOVEMBER 14, 1936**

  Arkansas-SMU Kern Tips/Bill Hightower

  TCU-Centenary Cy Leland/Bill Ware

- **NOVEMBER 21, 1936**

  SMU-Baylor Cy Leland/Gene Wyatt

  TCU-Rice Kern Tips/Bill Hightower

- **NOVEMBER 26, 1936**

  Texas A&M-Texas Kern Tips/Cy Leland

- **NOVEMBER 28, 1936**

  TCU-SMU Kern Tips/Bill Hightower

  Baylor-Rice Cy Leland/Gene Wyatt

- **DECEMBER 5, 1936**

  Texas-Arkansas Kern Tips/Bill Hightower

  SMU-Rice Cy Leland/Gene Wyatt

1937

- **SEPTEMBER 25, 1937**

  Texas Tech-Texas Kern Tips/Gene Wyatt

- **OCTOBER 2, 1937**

  TCU-Arkansas Kern Tips/Gene Wyatt

  Centenary-SMU Hal Thompson/Jack Mitchell

  Rice-Oklahoma Gene Cagle/Eddie Gallaher

  Texas-LSU Cy Leland/Bill Hightower

- **OCTOBER 16, 1937**

  Arkansas-Texas Cy Leland/Bill Hightower

  Texas A&M-TCU Kern Tips/Gene Wyatt

  Tulsa-Rice Gene Cagle/Tom Jacobs

  Vanderbilt-SMU Hal Thompson/Jack Mitchell

- **OCTOBER 23, 1937**

  Baylor-Texas A&M Kern Tips

  Rice-Texas Cy Leland

  SMU-Arkansas Gene Cagle

- **OCTOBER 30, 1937**

  TCU-Baylor Kern Tips/Gene Wyatt

  Auburn-Rice Eddie Gallaher/Tom Jacobs

  Texas A&M-Arkansas Cy Leland

  Texas-SMU Hal Thompson/Bill Hightower

- **NOVEMBER 6, 1937**

  Arkansas-Rice Kern Tips/Gene Wyatt

  SMU-Texas A&M Cy Leland/Jack Mitchell

  Texas-Baylor Hal Thompson/Bill Hightower

- **NOVEMBER 13, 1937**

  Texas A&M-Rice Kern Tips/Gene Wyatt

  TCU-Texas Cy Leland/Jack Mitchell

  Baylor-SMU Gene Cagle/Bill Hightower

- **NOVEMBER 20, 1937**

  Rice-TCU Kern Tips/Gene Wyatt

  Loyola-Baylor Cy Leland/Jack Mitchell

- **NOVEMBER 25, 1937**

  Texas-Texas A&M Kern Tips/Gene Wyatt

- **NOVEMBER 27, 1937**

  SMU-TCU Cy Leland/Hal Thompson

  Baylor-Rice Kern Tips/Gene Wyatt

- **DECEMBER 4, 1937**

  Rice-SMU Kern Tips/Gene Wyatt

- **JANUARY 1, 1938**

  Cotton Bowl

  Rice-Colorado Kern Tips/Gene Wyatt

1938

- **SEPTEMBER 24, 1938**

  Texas-Kansas Kern Tips/Gene Wyatt

  TCU-Centenary Cy Leland/Ves Box

- **OCTOBER 1, 1938**

  LSU-Texas Kern Tips/Pat Flaherty

  Oklahoma-Rice Ves Box/Gene Cagle

  Arizona-SMU Eddie Dunn/Jack Mitchell

  Tulsa-Texas A&M Cy Leland/Harfield Weedin

  Arkansas-TCU Hal Thompson/David Byrn

- **OCTOBER 7, 1938**

  TCU-Temple Cy Leland

- **OCTOBER 8, 1938**

  Texas A&M-Santa Clara Ves Box

  Rice-LSU Kern Tips/Jack Flaherty

- **OCTOBER 15, 1938**

  TCU-Texas A&M Kern Tips/Hal Thompson

  Texas-Arkansas Eddie Dunn/Gene Cagle

  Rice-Tulane Cy Leland/Harfield Weedin

  Centenary-Baylor Ves Box/Jack Mitchell

- **OCTOBER 22, 1938**

  SMU-Pittsburgh Hal Thompson

  Texas A&M-Baylor Kern Tips/Eddie Dunn

  Texas-Rice Cy Leland/Harfield Weedin

- **OCTOBER 29, 1938**

  Baylor-TCU Kern Tips/Hal Thompson

  Arkansas-Texas A&M Cy Leland/Harfield Weedin

  SMU-Texas Eddie Dunn/Bob Tongo

  Auburn-Rice Ves Box/Gene Cagle

- **NOVEMBER 5, 1938**
  Rice-Arkansas Kern Tips/Gene Wyatt
  Texas A&M-SMU Hal Thompson/Bud Sherman
  Baylor-Texas Eddie Dunn/Gene Cagle
  TCU-Tulsa Cy Leland/Harfield Weedin

- **NOVEMBER 12, 1938**
  Texas-TCU Kern Tips/Bud Sherman
  Rice-Texas A&M Hal Thompson/Harfield Weedin
  Arkansas-SMU Eddie Dunn/Gene Cagle
  Baylor-Loyola (Ca). Cy Leland

- **NOVEMBER 19, 1938**
  TCU-Rice Kern Tips/Hal Thompson
  SMU-Baylor Cy Leland/Eddie Dunn

- **NOVEMBER 24, 1938**
  Texas A&M-Texas Kern Tips/Hal Thompson

- **NOVEMBER 26, 1938**
  TCU-SMU Kern Tips
  Rice-Baylor Cy Leland

- **JANUARY 2, 1939**
  Cotton Bowl
  Texas Tech-St. Mary's Kern Tips/Hal Thompson

1939

- **SEPTEMBER 30, 1939**

  SMU-Oklahoma Cy Leland

  Florida-Texas Kern Tips/Conrad Brady

  Centenary-Texas A&M Eddie Dunn/Buddy Bostick

  Rice-Vanderbilt Hal Thompson/Harfield Weedin

- **OCTOBER 7, 1939**

  TCU-Arkansas Cy Leland

  Texas-Wisconsin Kern Tips

  Centenary-Rice Eddie Dunn

- **OCTOBER 14, 1939**

  Rice-LSU Kern Tips/Harfield Weedin

- **OCTOBER 21, 1939**

  Texas A&M-TCU Kern Tips/Harfield Weedin

  Baylor-Nebraska Cy Leland

  Arkansas-Texas Eddie Dunn/Dave Young

  Marquette-SMU Hal Thompson/Dan Riss

- **OCTOBER 28, 1939**

  Rice-Texas Cy Leland/Eddie Dunn

  Baylor-Texas A&M Kern Tips/Hal Thompson

- **NOVEMBER 4, 1939**

  Rice-Fordham Cy Leland

  Texas A&M-Arkansas Eddie Dunn/Harfield Weedin

  Texas-SMU Kern Tips/Dan Riss

  TCU-Baylor Hal Thompson/Dave Young

- **NOVEMBER 11, 1939**

  SMU-Texas A&M Kern Tips/Dan Riss

  Texas-Baylor Cy Leland/Buddy Bostick

  Arkansas-Rice Eddie Dunn/Harfield Weedin

  Tulsa-TCU Hal Thompson/Bud Sherman

- **NOVEMBER 18, 1939**
  Texas A&M-Rice Kern Tips/Dan Riss
  TCU-Texas Cy Leland/Dave Young
  SMU-Arkansas

- **NOVEMBER 25, 1939**
  Baylor-SMU Kern Tips/Hal Thompson
  Rice-TCU Cy Leland/Eddie Dunn

- **NOVEMBER 30, 1939**
  Texas-Texas A&M Kern Tips/Cy Leland

- **DECEMBER 2, 1939**
  SMU-TCU Kern Tips/Hal Thompson
  Baylor-Rice Cy Leland/Eddie Dunn

- **DECEMBER 9, 1939**
  Rice-SMU Kern Tips

1940

- **SEPTEMBER 28, 1940**
  Centenary-TCU Cy Leland/Ves Box
  Colorado-Texas Kern Tips/Dave Young

- **OCTOBER 5, 1940**
  Arkansas-TCU Kern Tips
  Tulsa-Texas A&M Cy Leland/Tee Casper
  Texas-Indiana Dan Riss/Dave Young
  Centenary-Rice Hal Thompson/Ves Box

- **OCTOBER 12, 1940**
  Texas-Oklahoma Cy Leland/Tee Casper
  SMU-Pittsburgh Dan Riss/Dave Young
  Baylor-Arkansas Ves Box/Tom Jacobs
  Texas A&M-UCLA Kern Tips
  LSU-Rice Hal Thompson/Pat Flaherty

- **OCTOBER 19, 1940**
  TCU-Texas A&M Kern Tips/Pat Flaherty
  Texas-Arkansas Cy Leland/Buddy Bostick
  Rice-Tulane Hal Thompson/Tom Jacobs
  Auburn-SMU Ves Box/Dave Russell
  Villanova-Baylor Dave Young

- **OCTOBER 26, 1940**
  Texas A&M-Baylor Hal Thompson/Tee Casper
  Texas-Rice Kern Tips/Dave Young
  TCU-Tulsa Cy Leland/Ves Box

- **NOVEMBER 2, 1940**
  Baylor-TCU Hal Thompson
  SMU-Texas Kern Tips
  Arkansas-Texas A&M Cy Leland
  Texas A&I-Rice Ves Box

- **NOVEMBER 9, 1940**
  Texas A&M-SMU Kern Tips/Tee Casper
  Baylor-Texas Hal Thompson/Dave Young
  Rice-Arkansas Cy Leland/Ves Box

- **NOVEMBER 16, 1940**
  Rice-Texas A&M Kern Tips/Pat Flaherty
  Arkansas-SMU Cy Leland/Bill Karn
  Texas-TCU Ves Box/Tee Casper

- **NOVEMBER 23, 1940**
  SMU-Baylor Cy Leland/Hal Thompson
  TCU-Rice Kern Tips

- **NOVEMBER 28, 1940**
  Texas A&M-Texas Kern Tips/Cy Leland

- **DECEMBER 7, 1940**
  SMU-Rice Kern Tips/Cy Leland

- **JANUARY 1, 1941**
  Cotton Bowl Fordham-Texas A&M Kern Tips/Cy Leland

1941

- **SEPTEMBER 27, 1941**
  Stanford-Baylor Cy Leland
  Colorado-Texas Kern Tips

- **OCTOBER 4, 1941**
  TCU-Arkansas Cy Leland/Ves Box
  LSU-Texas Kern Tips/Hal Thompson
  SMU-Fordham Dan Riss

- **OCTOBER 11, 1941**
  Texas-Oklahoma Kern Tips/Tee Casper
  Texas A&M-NYU Dan Riss
  Arkansas-Baylor Dave Young/Dave Byrn
  Tulane-Rice Hal Thompson/Bill Karn
  College of Pacific-SMU Ves Box/Dave Russell
  TCU-Indiana Cy Leland

- **OCTOBER 18, 1941**
  Texas A&M-TCU Kern Tips/Tee Casper
  Arkansas-Texas Ves Box/Dave Russell
  SMU-Auburn Cy Leland
  Rice-LSU Hal Thompson/Bill Karn

- **OCTOBER 25, 1941**
  Baylor-Texas A&M Cy Leland/Ves Box
  Rice-Texas Kern Tips/Hal Thompson
  TCU-Fordham Dan Riss

- **NOVEMBER 1, 1941**
  Texas-SMU Kern Tips/Hal Thompson
  TCU-Baylor Ves Box/Dave Russell
  Texas A&M-Arkansas Cy Leland/Tee Casper

- **NOVEMBER 8, 1941**
  SMU-Texas A&M Kern Tips/Tee Casper
  Texas-Baylor Hal Thompson /Dave Russell
  Arkansas-Rice Cy Leland/Bill Karn

- **NOVEMBER 22, 1941**
Rice-TCU Kern Tips/Tee Casper
Baylor-SMU Cy Leland/Hal Thompson

- **NOVEMBER 27, 1941**
Texas-Texas A&M Kern Tips/Cy Leland

- **NOVEMBER 29, 1941**
SMU-TCU Kern Tips/Tee Casper
Baylor-Rice Cy Leland/Hal Thompson

- **DECEMBER 6, 1941**
Rice-SMU Hal Thompson/Bill Karn
Oregon-Texas Kern Tips
Texas A&M-Washington State Cy Leland

- **JANUARY 1, 1942**
Cotton Bowl
Alabama-Texas A&M Kern Tips/Cy Leland

1942

- **SEPTEMBER 25, 1942**
TCU-UCLA Charlie Jordan

- **SEPTEMBER 26, 1942**
Kansas-Texas Kern Tips/Dave Byrn
Texas A&M-LSU Ves Box/Bill Newkirk
U.S. Naval Air Station-Rice Bill Michaels/Dave Russell

- **OCTOBER 3, 1942**
SMU-Pittsburgh Dan Riss
Texas-Northwestern Kern Tips
Texas Tech-Texas A&M Ves Box/Dave Russell
Arkansas-TCU /Bill Newkirk

- **OCTOBER 10, 1942**

  Baylor-Arkansas Charlie Jordan/Buddy Bostick

  Texas-Oklahoma Kern Tips/Harfield Weedin

  Texas A&M-Corpus Christi Naval Air Station
      Bill Michaels/Tom Jacobs

  Rice-Tulane Ves Box/Bill Newkirk

  Kansas-TCU Dave Russell/Dave Byrn

  Texas A&M-LSU Ves Box/Bill Michaels

  Corpus Christi Naval Air Station-Rice Bill Michaels

- **OCTOBER 17, 1942**

  Texas-Arkansas Ves Box/Buddy Bostick

  TCU-Texas A&M Kern Tips/Dave Russell

- **OCTOBER 24, 1942**

  Texas-Rice Kern Tips/Bill Newkirk

  Texas A&M-Baylor Ves Box/Bill Michaels

  Corpus Christi Naval Air Station-SMU
      Charlie Jordan/Dave Russell

- **OCTOBER 31, 1942**

  Texas Tech-Rice Bill Michaels/Bill Newkirk

  Arkansas-Texas A&M Charlie Jordan/Dave Byrn

  Baylor-TCU Kern Tips/Harfield Weedin

  SMU-Texas Ves Box/Dave Russell

- **NOVEMBER 7, 1942**

  Baylor-Texas Kern Tips/Harfield Weedin

  Texas A&M-SMU Bill Michaels/Bill Newkirk

  Rice-Arkansas Charlie Jordan/Buddy Bostick

  TCU-Texas Tech Ves Box/Dave Russell

- **NOVEMBER 14, 1942**
  Texas-TCU Kern Tips/Dave Byrn
  Texas A&M-Rice Ves Box/Bill Newkirk
  Arkansas-SMU Charlie Jordan/Dave Russell
  Baylor-Tulsa Bill Michaels/Buddy Bostick

- **NOVEMBER 21, 1942**
  SMU-Baylor Ves Box/Dave Russell
  TCU-Rice Kern Tips/Bill Newkirk

- **NOVEMBER 28, 1942**
  TCU-SMU Kern Tips/Dave Russell
  Rice-Baylor Ves Box/Charlie Jordan

- **DECEMBER 6, 1942**
  SMU-Rice Ves Box/Dave Russell
  Washington State-Texas A&M Kern Tips/Bill Michaels

1943

- **OCTOBER 2, 1943**
  Southwestern-Texas Kern Tips/Harfield Weedin
  TCU-Arkansas Charlie Jordan/Dave Byrn
  North Texas Agricultural College-SMU
      Dave Russell/Buddy Bostick
  Texas Tech-Texas A&M Bill Michaels/Pat Flaherty
  Rice-LSU Ves Box/Tom Jacobs

- **OCTOBER 9, 1943**
  Texas-Oklahoma Kern Tips/Dave Russell
  Rice-Tulane Ves Box/Tom Jacobs
  Texas A&M-LSU Bill Michaels/Ted Nabors
  SMU-Naval Air Technical Training
      Charlie Jordan/Buddy Bostick

- **OCTOBER 16, 1943**
  Texas A&M-TCU Kern Tips/Dave Russell
  Rice-SMU Ves Box/Buddy Bostick
  Arkansas-Texas Bill Michaels/Harfield Weedin

- **OCTOBER 23, 1943**
  Rice-Texas Kern Tips/Harfield Weedin
  Texas A&M-North Texas Dave Russell/Buddy Bostick
  SMU-Tulane Ves Box/Tom Jacobs
  TCU-Oklahoma A&M Charlie Jordan
  Southwestern University-Southwestern Louisiana Institute
     Bill Michaels/Pat Flaherty

- **OCTOBER 30, 1943**
  Texas A&M-Arkansas Ves Box/Dave Russell
  Rice-Texas Tech Bill Michaels/Pat Flaherty
  Texas-SMU Kern Tips/Bob Holton
  TCU-LSU Charlie Jordan/Buddy Bostick

- **NOVEMBER 6, 1943**
  TCU-Texas Tech Charlie Jordan/Buddy Bostick
  SMU-Texas A&M- Kern Tips/Dave Russell
  Arkansas-Rice Ves Box/Harfield Weedin

- **NOVEMBER 13, 1943**
  TCU-Texas Kern Tips/Harfield Weedin
  Arkansas-SMU Bill Michaels/Dave Russell (San Antonio)
  Texas A&M-Rice Ves Box/Charlie Jordan

- **NOVEMBER 20, 1943**
  Rice-TCU Kern Tips/Bill Michaels
  Texas Tech-SMU Ves Box/Bob Holton

- **NOVEMBER 27, 1943**
  Rice-Southwestern Kern Tips/Bill Michaels
  SMU-TCU Ves Box/Charlie Jordan

- **JANUARY 1, 1944**
  Texas-Randolph Field—Kern Tips/Ves Box

1944

- **SEPTEMBER 30, 1944**

Texas-Southwestern Kern Tips/Dave Russell
SMU-North Texas Agricultural College Charlie Jordan/Fred Kincaid
Texas A&M-Texas Tech Bill Michaels/Alec Chesser—
    (Chesser's first game) in San Antonio
Rice-Randolph Field Ves Box/Fred Nahas

- **OCTOBER 7, 1944**

Arkansas-TCU Charlie Jordan/Fred Kincaid
Randolph Field-Texas Kern Tips/Dick Lyons
Southwestern-SMU Dave Russell/Jerry Doggett
LSU-Rice Bill Michaels/Fred Nahas
Texas A&M-Oklahoma Ves Box/George Harding

- **OCTOBER 14, 1944**

Texas-Oklahoma Kern Tips/Jerry Doggett
Tulane-Rice Dave Russell/Fred Nahas
SMU-Randolph Field Bill Michaels/Alec Chesser
Texas A&M-LSU Ves Box/Charlie Jordan

- **OCTOBER 21, 1944**

TCU-Texas A&M Kern Tips/Dave Russell
Texas-Arkansas Ves Box/Charlie Jordan
SMU-Rice Bill Michaels/Fred Nahas

- **OCTOBER 28, 1944**

Texas A&M-North Texas Dave Russell/Fred Kincaid
Texas-Rice Kern Tips/Fred Nahas
SMU-Tulane Ves Box/Bill Michaels
TCU-Oklahoma Charlie Jordan/Jerry Doggett

- **NOVEMBER 4, 1944**

Rice-Texas Tech Charlie Jordan/Fred Nahas
SMU-Texas Kern Tips/Bill Michaels
Arkansas-Texas A&M Ves Box/Dave Russell

- **NOVEMBER 11, 1944**
  Rice-Arkansas Charlie Jordan/Dave Russell
  Texas A&M-SMU Kern Tips/Fred Kincaid
  TCU-Texas Tech Bill Michaels/Jerry Doggett
  Texas-Oklahoma A&M Ves Box/Fred Nahas

- **NOVEMBER 18, 1944**
  Arkansas-SMU Bill Michaels/Jerry Doggett
  Texas-TCU Ves Box/Dave Russell
  Texas A&M-Rice Kern Tips/Fred Nahas

- **NOVEMBER 25, 1944**
  TCU-Rice Kern Tips/Charlie Jordan
  SMU-Texas Tech Ves Box/Dave Russell

- **NOVEMBER 30, 1944**
  Texas A&M-Texas Kern Tips/Ves Box/Charlie Jordan

- **DECEMBER 2, 1944**
  TCU-SMU Kern Tips/Bill Michaels
  Southwestern-Rice Ves Box/Fred Nahas

- **JANUARY 1, 1945**
  Cotton Bowl
  TCU-Oklahoma A&M Kern Tips/Ves Box

1945

- **SEPTEMBER 29, 1945**
  TCU-Baylor Kern Tips/Dave Russell
  Southwestern-Texas Charlie Jordan/Fred Kincaid
  Texas A&M-Texas Tech Ves Box/Alec Chesser
  Rice-LSU Bill Michaels/Francis Siebert

- **OCTOBER 6, 1945**
  TCU-Arkansas Kern Tips/Alec Chesser
  Texas A&M-Oklahoma Charlie Jordan/Fritz Kuler
  Missouri-SMU Ves Box/Fred Kincaid
  Texas Tech-Texas Bill Michaels/Dick Bush
  Southwestern-Rice Ves Box/Fred Kincaid

- **OCTOBER 12, 1945**

  SMU-Oklahoma A&M Dave Russell/Dick Bush

- **OCTOBER 13, 1945**

  Texas-Oklahoma Kern Tips/Fred Kincaid
  Tulane-Rice Ves Box/Fred Nahas
  Texas A&M-LSU Bill Michaels/Tom Holbrook

- **OCTOBER 20, 1945**

  Texas-Arkansas Kern Tips/Dave Russell
  Texas A&M-TCU Ves Box/Dick Bush
  Rice-SMU Charlie Jordan/Fred Kincaid
  Baylor-Texas Tech Bill Michaels/Alec Chesser

- **OCTOBER 27, 1945**

  Rice-Texas Kern Tips/Alec Chesser
  Baylor-Texas A&M Charlie Jordan/Dick Bush
  SMU-Tulane Ves Box/Dave Russell
  Oklahoma A&M-TCU Bill Michaels/Fred Kincaid

- **NOVEMBER 3, 1945**

  Texas-SMU Kern Tips/Fred Kincaid
  Texas A&M-Arkansas Ves Box/Alec Chesser
  TCU-Oklahoma Charlie Jordan/Francis Gilbert
  Southwestern-Baylor Bill Michaels/Dick Bush
  Texas Tech-Rice Dave Russell/Fred Nahas

- **NOVEMBER 10, 1945**

  Baylor-Texas Charlie Jordan/Jerry Doggett
  SMU-Texas A&M Ves Box/Dick Bush
  TCU-Texas Tech Dave Russell/Alec Chesser
  Arkansas-Rice Kern Tips/Bill Michaels

- **NOVEMBER 17, 1945**

  TCU-Texas Kern Tips/Jerry Doggett
  Texas A&M-Rice Ves Box/Dave Russell
  Arkansas-SMU Charlie Jordan/Dick Bush
  Baylor-Tulsa Bill Michaels/Alec Chesser

- **NOVEMBER 24, 1945**
  Rice-TCU Kern Tips/Dave Russell
  SMU-Baylor Ves Box/Charlie Jordan

- **NOVEMBER 29, 1945**
  Texas-Texas A&M Kern Tips

- **DECEMBER 1, 1945**
  Baylor-Rice Kern Tips/Fred Nahas
  SMU-TCU Ves Box/Jerry Doggett

- **JANUARY 1, 1946**
  Cotton Bowl
  Texas-Missouri Kern Tips/Bill Michaels
  Oil Bowl
  Georgia-Tulsa Ves Box/Jerry Doggett

1946

- **SEPTEMBER 21, 1946**
  Missouri-Texas Kern Tips/Alec Chesser

- **SEPTEMBER 27, 1946**
  SMU-Temple Charlie Jordan

- **SEPTEMBER 28, 1946**
  Baylor-TCU Kern Tips/Alec Chesser
  Colorado-Texas Hal Thompson/Dick Lyons
  Texas Tech-Texas A&M Ves Box/Fred Kincaid
  LSU-Rice Bill Michaels/Dave Russell

- **OCTOBER 5, 1946**
  Arkansas-TCU Bill Michaels/Bill Hightower
  Oklahoma A&M-Texas Kern Tips/Alec Chesser
  Texas A&M-Oklahoma Ves Box/Fred Kincaid
  Texas Tech-SMU Charlie Jordan/Jerry Doggett

- **OCTOBER 11, 1946**
TCU-Miami Bill Michaels/Bill Hightower
Oklahoma State-SMU Charlie Jordan/Bill Michaels

- **OCTOBER 12, 1946**
Baylor-Arkansas Kern Tips/Alec Chesser
Texas A&M-LSU Hal Thompson/Dick Lyons

- **OCTOBER 19, 1946**
Arkansas-Texas Kern Tips/Alec Chesser
Baylor-Texas Tech Bill Michaels
TCU-Texas A&M Ves Box/Fred Kincaid

- **OCTOBER 25, 1946**
TCU-Oklahoma A&M Bill Michaels/Bill Hightower

- **OCTOBER 26, 1946**
Texas-Rice Kern Tips/Alec Chesser
Texas A&M-Baylor Charlie Jordan/Jerry Doggett
SMU-Missouri Ves Box/Fred Kincaid

- **NOVEMBER 2, 1946**
SMU-Texas Kern Tips/Alec Chesser
Arkansas-Texas A&M Ves Box/Fred Kincaid

- **NOVEMBER 9, 1946**
Rice-Arkansas Kern Tips/Alec Chesser
Texas A&M-SMU Ves Box/Fred Kincaid

- **NOVEMBER 16, 1946**
Rice-Texas A&M Kern Tips/Alec Chesser
Texas-TCU Charlie Jordan/Jerry Doggett
SMU-Arkansas Ves Box/Fred Kincaid
Baylor-Tulsa Bill Michaels/Bill Hightower

- **NOVEMBER 23, 1946**
Baylor-SMU Charlie Jordan/Jerry Doggett
TCU-Rice Kern Tips/Alec Chesser

- **NOVEMBER 28, 1946**
  Texas A&M-Texas Kern Tips/Alec Chesser

- **NOVEMBER 30, 1946**
  TCU-SMU Ves Box/Fred Kincaid
  Baylor-Rice Kern Tips/Alec Chesser

- **JANUARY 1, 1947**
  Cotton Bowl
  Arkansas-LSU Kern Tips/Alec Chesser
  Oil Bowl St. Mary's-Georgia Tech Ves Box/Fred Kincaid

1947

- **SEPTEMBER 20, 1947**
  Texas-Texas Tech Kern Tips/Alec Chesser
  TCU-Kansas Charlie Jordan

- **SEPTEMBER 26, 1947**
  Baylor-Miami Ves Box

- **SEPTEMBER 27, 1947**
  Texas-Oregon Kern Tips
  Oklahoma A&M-TCU Fred Kincaid/Bill Newkirk
  SMU-Santa Clara Charlie Jordan
  Texas Tech-Texas A&M Jerry Doggett/Eddie Barker
  Rice-LSU Bill Michaels/Alec Chesser

- **OCTOBER 4, 1947**
  TCU-Arkansas Jerry Doggett/Fred Kincaid
  Rice-USC Kern Tips
  North Carolina-Texas Ves Box
  Texas A&M-Oklahoma Charlie Jordan/Eddie Barker
  Missouri-SMU Bill Michaels/Alec Chesser

- **OCTOBER 10, 1947**
  TCU-Miami Charlie Jordan

- **OCTOBER 11, 1947**

  Texas-Oklahoma Kern Tips/Alec Chesser

  SMU-Oklahoma A&M Jerry Doggett/Gene Heard

  Texas A&M-LSU Bill Michaels/Gordon McLendon

  Rice-Tulane Ves Box/Bill Newkirk

  Arkansas-Baylor Fred Kincaid/Eddie Barker

- **OCTOBER 18, 1947**

  Texas A&M-TCU Charlie Jordan/Jerry Doggett

  Texas-Arkansas Ves Box/Fred Kincaid (Memphis)

  Rice-SMU Kern Tips/Alec Chesser

- **OCTOBER 25, 1947**

  Rice-Texas Kern Tips/Alec Chesser

  SMU-UCLA Ves Box

  Baylor-Texas A&M Charlie Jordan/Jerry Doggett

  TCU-Oklahoma Bill Michaels/Fred Kincaid

- **NOVEMBER 1, 1947**

  Texas-SMU Kern Tips/Alec Chesser

  TCU-Baylor Bill Michaels/Eddie Barker

  Texas A&M-Arkansas Ves Box/Fred Kincaid

  Texas Tech-Rice Charlie Jordan/Jerry Doggett

- **NOVEMBER 8, 1947**

  Baylor-Texas Kern Tips/Alec Chesser

  SMU-Texas A&M Charlie Jordan/Jerry Doggett

  Arkansas-Rice Ves Box/Fred Kincaid

- **NOVEMBER 15, 1947**

  TCU-Texas Ves Box/Eddie Barker

  Arkansas-SMU Charlie Jordan/Alex Chesser

  Texas A&M-Rice Bill Michaels/Bill Newkirk

- **NOVEMBER 22, 1947**

  Rice-TCU Ves Box/Fred Kincaid

  SMU-Baylor Charlie Jordan/Jerry Doggett

- **NOVEMBER 27, 1947**

  Texas-Texas A&M Kern Tips

- **NOVEMBER 29, 1947**

  SMU-TCU Kern Tips/Alec Chesser

  Baylor-Rice Charlie Jordan/Jerry Doggett

- **JANUARY 1, 1948**

  Cotton Bowl

  Penn State-SMU Kern Tips/Alec Chesser

1948

- **SEPTEMBER 18, 1948**

  Texas A&M-Villanova Charlie Jordan

  LSU-Texas Kern Tips/Alec Chesser

  TCU-Kansas Bill Michaels/Jerry Doggett

- **SEPTEMBER 25, 1948**

  SMU-Pittsburgh Charlie Jordan

  Texas-North Carolina Kern Tips

  TCU-Oklahoma State Ves Box/Fred Kincaid

  Tulsa-Baylor Eddie Barker/Buddy Bostick

  Texas A&M-Texas Tech Bill Michaels/Alec Chesser

  Sam Houston State-Rice Jerry Doggett/Bill Newkirk

- **OCTOBER 2, 1948**

  New Mexico-Texas Bill Michaels/Alec Chesser

  Baylor-Mississippi State Ed Dittert/Buddy Bostick

  Texas Tech-SMU Charlie Jordan/Fred Kincaid

  Texas A&M-Oklahoma Kern Tips

  Arkansas-TCU Eddie Barker/Hal Thompson

  LSU-Rice Ves Box/Bill Newkirk

- **OCTOBER 9, 1948**
  Rice-USC Ves Box
  Texas A&M-LSU Bill Michaels/Bill Newkirk
  Baylor-Arkansas Ed Dittert/Fred Kincaid
  Texas-Oklahoma Kern Tips/Alec Chesser
  TCU-Indiana Eddie Barker/Hal Thompson
  SMU-Missouri Charlie Jordan

- **OCTOBER 16, 1948**
  Arkansas-Texas Charlie Jordan/Fred Kincaid
  TCU-Texas A&M Ves Box/Jerry Doggett
  Texas Tech-Baylor Bill Michaels/Eddie Barker
  SMU-Rice Kern Tips/Alec Chesser

- **OCTOBER 23, 1948**
  Texas-Rice Kern Tips/Alec Chesser
  Texas A&M-Baylor Bill Michaels/Eddie Barker
  Oklahoma-TCU Charlie Jordan/Hal Thompson
  Santa Clara-SMU Ves Box/Fred Kincaid

- **OCTOBER 30, 1948**
  SMU-Texas Kern Tips/Alec Chesser
  Rice-Texas Tech Bill Michaels/Eddie Barker
  Arkansas-Texas A&M Ves Box/Fred Kincaid
  Baylor-TCU Charlie Jordan/Jerry Doggett

- **NOVEMBER 6, 1948**
  Rice-Arkansas Ves Box/Fred Kincaid
  Texas A&M-SMU Kern Tips

- **NOVEMBER 13, 1948**
  Texas-TCU Kern Tips/Alec Chesser
  SMU-Arkansas Charlie Jordan/Hal Thompson
  Baylor-Tulane Bill Michaels/Eddie Barker
  Rice-Texas A&M Ves Box/Fred Kincaid

- **NOVEMBER 20, 1948**
  Baylor-SMU Kern Tips/Alec Chesser
  TCU-Rice Ves Box/Jerry Doggett

- **NOVEMBER 25, 1948**
  Texas A&M-Texas Kern Tips/Alec Chesser

- **NOVEMBER 27, 1948**
  TCU-SMU Charlie Jordan/Jerry Doggett
  Rice-Baylor Ves Box/Alec Chesser

- **JANUARY 1, 1949**
  Cotton Bowl
  Oregon-SMU Kern Tips/Alec Chesser

1949

- **SEPTEMBER 17, 1949**
  Texas Tech-Texas Kern Tips/Alec Chesser
  TCU-Kansas Charlie Jordan/Jerry Doggett
  Villanova-Texas A&M Ves Box/Fred Kincaid

- **SEPTEMBER 24, 1949**
  Texas-Temple Ves Box
  Wake Forest-SMU Kern Tips
  Rice-Clemson Eddie Barker
  TCU-Oklahoma A&M Charlie Jordan
  Baylor-South Carolina Dave Russell
  Texas Tech-Texas A&M Bill Michaels

- **OCTOBER 1, 1949**
  TCU-Arkansas Charlie Jordan/Fred Kincaid
  Idaho-Texas Eddie Barker/Alec Chesser
  Missouri-SMU Ves Box/Hal Thompson
  Baylor-Mississippi State Dave Russell/Buddy Bostick
  LSU-Rice Bill Michaels/Jim Wiggins

- **OCTOBER 8, 1949**
  Arkansas-Baylor Bill Michaels//Buddy Bostick
  Texas-Oklahoma Kern Tips/Alec Chesser
  Texas A&M-LSU Ves Box/Hal Thompson
  TCU-Indiana Charlie Jordan/Fred Kinkaid
  New Mexico-Rice Eddie Barker/Bill Newkirk

- **OCTOBER 15, 1949**
  Rice-SMU Kern Tips/Alec Chesser
  Texas-Arkansas Charlie Jordan/Hal Thompson
  Texas A&M-TCU Bill Michaels/Fred Kincaid
  Baylor-Texas Tech Eddie Barker/Buddy Bostick

- **OCTOBER 22, 1949**
  Rice-Texas Kern Tips/Alec Chesser
  Baylor-Texas A&M Bill Michaels/Eddie Barker
  Kentucky-SMU Ves Box/Fred Kincaid
  Mississippi-TCU Charlie Jordan/Hal Thompson

- **OCTOBER 29, 1949**
  Texas-SMU Kern Tips/Alec Chesser
  TCU-Baylor Charlie Jordan/Fred Kincaid
  Texas A&M-Arkansas Ves Box/Hal Thompson
  Texas Tech-Rice Bill Michaels/Eddie Barker

- **NOVEMBER 5, 1949**
  Baylor-Texas Kern Tips/Alec Chesser
  SMU-Texas A&M Ves Box/Jerry Doggett
  Arkansas-Rice Charlie Jordan/Fred Kincaid

- **NOVEMBER 12, 1949**
  Arkansas-SMU Kern Tips/Alec Chesser
  Texas A&M-Rice Charlie Jordan/Fred Kincaid
  TCU-Texas Ves Box/Eddie Barker
  Wyoming-Baylor Bill Michaels/Buddy Bostick

- **NOVEMBER 19, 1949**
  SMU-Baylor Kern Tips/Alec Chesser
  Rice-TCU Ves Box/Eddie Barker

- **NOVEMBER 24, 1949**
  Texas-Texas A&M Kern Tips/Alec Chesser

- **DECEMBER 3, 1949**
  Notre Dame-SMU Kern Tips/Alec Chesser

- **JANUARY 2, 1950**
  Cotton Bowl
  Kern Tips/Alec Chesser

1950

- **SEPTEMBER 23, 1950**
  Georgia Tech-SMU Kern Tips/Alec Chesser
  TCU-Kansas Ves Box/Dave Russell
  Texas-Texas Tech Charlie Jordan/Eddie Barker
  Texas A&M-Nevada Jerry Doggett/Bob Walker
  Baylor-Wyoming Bill Michaels/Buddy Bostick

- **SEPTEMBER 30, 1950**
  Purdue-Texas Kern Tips/Alec Chesser
  SMU-Ohio State Ves Box/Buddy Bostick
  TCU-Oklahoma A&M Jerry Doggett
  Houston-Baylor Charlie Jordan/Hal Thompson
  Rice-Santa Clara
  Texas Tech-Texas A&M Bill Michaels/Jim Wiggins

- **OCTOBER 7, 1950**
  Arkansas-TCU Charlie Jordan/Jerry Doggett
  Texas A&M-Oklahoma Kern Tips/Alec Chesser
  SMU-Missouri Ves Box/Dave Russell
  LSU-Rice Bill Michaels/Bob Walker
  Baylor-Mississippi State Eddie Barker/Buddy Bostick

- **OCTOBER 14, 1950**
  Texas-Oklahoma Kern Tips/Alec Chesser
  Rice-Pittsburgh Charlie Jordan/Buddy Bostick
  Baylor-Arkansas Eddie Barker/Jim Wiggins
  VMI-Texas A&M Bill Michaels/Bob Walker
  TCU-Texas Tech Dave Russell/Carl Mann
  SMU-Oklahoma A&M Ves Box/Alec Chesser

- **OCTOBER 21, 1950**
  TCU-Texas A&M Charlie Jordan/Dave Russell
  Arkansas-Texas Ves Box/Jerry Doggett
  Texas Tech-Baylor Bill Michaels/Eddie Barker
  SMU-Rice Kern Tips/Alec Chesser

- **OCTOBER 28, 1950**
  Texas-Rice Kern Tips/Alec Chesser
  Texas A&M-Baylor Ves Box/Buddy Bostick
  TCU-Mississippi Charlie Jordan/Dave Russell

- **NOVEMBER 4, 1950**
  SMU-Texas Kern Tips/Alec Chesser
  Arkansas-Texas A&M Charlie Jordan/Dave Russell
  Baylor-TCU Ves Box/Jerry Doggett
  Texas Tech-Rice Bill Michaels/Eddie Barker

- **NOVEMBER 11, 1950**
  Texas-Baylor Kern Tips/Alec Chesser
  Texas A&M-SMU Charlie Jordan/Bob Walker
  Rice-Arkansas Ves Box/Eddie Barker

- **NOVEMBER 18, 1950**
  Texas-TCU Ves Box/Dave Russell
  Rice-Texas A&M Kern Tips/Alec Chesser
  SMU-Arkansas Charlie Jordan/Buddy Bostick

- **NOVEMBER 25, 1950**
  TCU-Rice Ves Box/Jerry Doggett
  Baylor-SMU Kern Tips/Alec Chesser

- **NOVEMBER 30, 1950**

  Texas A&M-Texas Kern Tips/Alec Chesser

- **DECEMBER 2, 1950**

  TCU-SMU Kern Tips/Alec Chesser

  Rice-Baylor Charlie Jordan/Eddie Barker

- **DECEMBER 9, 1950**

  Texas A&M-Georgia Charlie Jordan/Eddie Barker

- **JANUARY 1, 1951**

  Cotton Bowl

  Tennessee-Texas Kern Tips/Alec Chesser

1951

- **SEPTEMBER 22, 1951**

  Texas A&M-UCLA Charlie Jordan/Eddie Barker

  SMU-Georgia Tech Ves Box/Jerry Doggett

  Kentucky-Texas Kern Tips/Alec Chesser

  Baylor-Houston John Ferguson/Dave Russell

  Kansas-TCU Bill Michaels/Bob Walker

- **SEPTEMBER 29, 1951**

  TCU-Nebraska Ves Box/Glenn Brown

  Texas A&M-Texas Tech John Ferguson/Alec Chesser

  Texas-Purdue Charlie Jordan/Bob Walker

  SMU-Ohio State Kern Tips/Eddie Barker

- **OCTOBER 6, 1951**

  Rice-LSU John Ferguson/Bob Walker

  North Carolina-Texas Charlie Jordan/Dave Smith

  Missouri-SMU Ves Box/Glenn Brown

  Oklahoma-Texas A&M Kern Tips/Alec Chesser

  TCU-Arkansas Dave Russell/Eddie Hill

- **OCTOBER 13, 1951**

  Arkansas-Baylor John Ferguson/Eddie Hill
  Texas-Oklahoma Kern Tips/Alec Chesser
  SMU-Notre Dame Charlie Jordan/Bob Walker
  TCU-Texas Tech Bill Michaels/Dave Smith
  Texas A&M-Trinity Dave Russell/Jim Wiggins
  Navy-Rice Ves Box/Glenn Brown

- **OCTOBER 20, 1951**

  Texas A&M-TCU Kern Tips/Alec Chesser
  Texas-Arkansas Ves Box/Dave Russell
  Texas Tech-Baylor Bill Michaels/Bob Walker
  Rice-SMU Charlie Jordan/John Ferguson

- **OCTOBER 27, 1951**

  Rice-Texas Kern Tips/Alec Chesser
  Baylor-Texas A&M Charlie Jordan/John Ferguson
  TCU-USC Ves Box/Eddie Barker

- **NOVEMBER 3, 1951**

  Texas A&M-Arkansas Charlie Jordan/Dave Russell
  TCU-Baylor Ves Box/John Ferguson
  Texas-SMU Kern Tips/Alec Chesser
  Rice-Pittsburgh Bill Michaels/Eddie Barker

- **NOVEMBER 10, 1951**

  Baylor-Texas Kern Tips/Alec Chesser
  SMU-Texas A&M Charlie Jordan/John Ferguson
  Arkansas-Rice Ves Box/Eddie Barker

- **NOVEMBER 17, 1951**

  TCU-Texas Kern Tips/Alec Chesser
  Arkansas-SMU Charlie Jordan/John Ferguson
  Texas A&M-Rice Ves Box/Dave Russell
  Wake Forest-Baylor Bill Michaels/Bob Walker

- **NOVEMBER 24, 1951**
  Rice-TCU Kern Tips/Alec Chesser
  SMU-Baylor Charlie Jordan/John Ferguson

- **NOVEMBER 29, 1951**
  Texas-Texas A&M Kern Tips/Alec Chesser

- **DECEMBER 1, 1951**
  SMU-TCU
  Baylor-Rice

- **JANUARY 1, 1952**
  Cotton Bowl
  Kentucky-TCU Kern Tips/Alec Chesser

1952

- **SEPTEMBER 20, 1952**
  TCU-Kansas Kern Tips/Alec Chesser
  Wake Forest-Baylor John Ferguson/Dave Russell
  Texas-LSU Charlie Jordan/Eddie Barker
  Texas A&M-Houston Ves Box/Bob Walker

- **SEPTEMBER 26, 1952**
  Duke-SMU Kern Tips/Alec Chesser

- **SEPTEMBER 27, 1952**
  Texas-North Carolina Ves Box/Dave Smith
  TCU-UCLA John Ferguson/Eddie Barker
  Texas A&M-Oklahoma A&M Charlie Jordan/Jerry Doggett
  Texas Tech-Rice Bob Walker/Dave Russell

- **OCTOBER 4, 1952**
  Notre Dame-Texas Kern Tips/Alec Chesser
  Washington State-Baylor Bob Walker/Jerry Doggett
  Kentucky-Texas A&M Ves Box/Dave Russell
  Arkansas-TCU Bill Michaels/Dave Smith
  Georgia Tech-SMU Charlie Jordan/Eddie Barker
  LSU-Rice John Ferguson/Coit Butler

- **OCTOBER 11, 1952**

  Texas A&M-Michigan State Ves Box/Eddie Barker

  Texas-Oklahoma Kern Tips/Alec Chesser

  SMU-Missouri Bob Walker/Jim Wiggins

  TCU-Trinity Bill Michaels/Coit Butler

- **OCTOBER 18, 1952**

  TCU-Texas A&M Kern Tips/Alec Chesser

  Arkansas-Texas Charlie Jordan/Eddie Barker

  Baylor-Texas Tech John Ferguson/Bob Walker

  SMU-Rice Ves Box/Dave Smith

- **OCTOBER 25, 1952**

  Texas A&M-Baylor Ves Box/Bob Walker

  Texas-Rice Kern Tips/Alec Chesser

  Kansas-SMU Charlie Jordan/John Ferguson

- **NOVEMBER 1, 1952**

  Baylor-TCU Ves Box/Bob Walker

  Wisconsin-Rice John Ferguson/Dave Russell

  SMU-Texas Kern Tips/Alec Chesser

  Arkansas-Texas A&M Charlie Jordan/Eddie Barker

- **NOVEMBER 8, 1952**

  Texas A&M-SMU Kern Tips/Alec Chesser

  Rice-Arkansas Ves Box/Eddie Barker

  Texas-Baylor Charlie Jordan/Bob Walker

  Wake Forest-TCU John Ferguson/Dave Russell

- **NOVEMBER 15, 1952**

  Texas-TCU Kern Tips/Alec Chesser

  Rice-Texas A&M Charlie Jordan/Bob Walker

  SMU-Arkansas Ves Box/Eddie Barker

  Baylor-Houston John Ferguson/Dave Russell

- **NOVEMBER 22, 1952**
  Baylor-SMU Kern Tips/Alec Chesser
  TCU-Rice Charlie Jordan/John Ferguson

- **NOVEMBER 27, 1952**
  Texas A&M-Texas Kern Tips/Alec Chesser

- **NOVEMBER 29, 1952**
  Rice-Baylor Ves Box/John Ferguson
  TCU-SMU Kern Tips/Alec Chesser

1953

- **SEPTEMBER 19, 1953**
  West Texas State College-Texas Tech Eddie Barker/Jack Dale
  Texas-LSU John Ferguson/Dave Smith
  Texas A&M-Kentucky Ves Box/Coit Butler
  Kansas-TCU Kern Tips/Alec Chesser
  Baylor-California Dave Russell/Joe Cullinane
  Florida-Rice Bob Walker/Eddie Hill

- **SEPTEMBER 26, 1953**
  Villanova-Texas Kern Tips/Alec Chesser
  Texas-Houston Ves Box/Bob Walker
  Texas Tech-Texas Western John Ferguson/Eddie Barker

- **OCTOBER 2, 1953**
  Baylor-Miami Bob Walker/Joe Cullinane

- **OCTOBER 3, 1953**
  Rice-Cornell Dave Russell/Coit Butler
  SMU-Georgia Tech Ves Box/Jerry Doggett
  TCU-Arkansas Bill Michaels/Jim Wiggins
  Georgia-Texas A&M Kern Tips/Alec Chesser

- **OCTOBER 9, 1953**
  Missouri-SMU Bob Walker/Jerry Doggett

- **OCTOBER 10, 1953**

  TCU-Michigan State Ves Box/Joe Cullinane
  Texas-Oklahoma Kern Tips/Alec Chesser
  Arkansas-Baylor Dave Russell/Eddie Hill
  Texas Tech-Texas A&M John Ferguson/Jack Dale
  Hardin-Simmons-Rice Eddie Barker/Dave Smith

- **OCTOBER 17, 1953**

  Texas A&M-TCU Kern Tips/Alec Chesser
  Texas-Arkansas John Ferguson/Eddie Barker
  Vanderbilt-Baylor Bob Walker/Jerry Doggett
  Rice-SMU Ves Box/Eddie Hill

- **OCTOBER 24, 1953**

  TCU-Penn State John Ferguson/Jerry Doggett
  Rice-Texas Kern Tips/Alec Chesser
  Baylor-Texas A&M Ves Box/Dave Smith
  Kansas-SMU Dave Russell/Eddie Barker
  New Mexico A&M-Texas Tech Bob Walker/Jack Dale

- **OCTOBER 31, 1953**

  Texas-SMU Kern Tips/Alec Chesser
  TCU-Baylor Ves Box/Coit Butler
  Texas Tech-Mississippi State Bob Walker/Jack Dale
  Texas A&M-Arkansas John Ferguson/Eddie Barker

- **NOVEMBER 7, 1953**

  Baylor-Texas Kern Tips/Alec Chesser
  SMU-Texas A&M Ves Box/Dave Smith
  TCU-Washington State Dave Russell/Eddie Barker
  Arkansas-Rice John Ferguson/Coit Butler

- **NOVEMBER 14, 1953**
  Texas A&M-Rice Ves Box/Dave Smith
  TCU-Texas Kern Tips/Alec Chesser
  Houston-Baylor Dave Russell/Eddie Hill
  Arkansas-SMU John Ferguson/Eddie Barker
  Texas Tech-Tulsa Bob Walker/Jack Dale

- **NOVEMBER 21, 1953**
  SMU-Baylor Kern Tips/Alec Chesser
  Rice-TCU Ves Box/Eddie Barker
  Texas Tech-Houston John Ferguson/Bob Walker

- **NOVEMBER 26, 1953**
  Texas-Texas A&M Kern Tips/Alec Chesser

- **NOVEMBER 28, 1953**
  SMU-TCU Ves Box/Bob Walker
  Baylor-Rice Kern Tips/Alec Chesser
  Hardin-Simmons-Texas Tech John Ferguson/Eddie Barker

- **DECEMBER 5, 1953**
  SMU-Notre Dame Kern Tips/Alec Chesser

1954

- **SEPTEMBER 18, 1954**
  LSU-Texas Kern Tips/Eddie Barker
  Houston-Baylor Dave Russell/Coit Butler
  TCU-Kansas Bob Walker/Jerry Doggett
  Florida-Rice John Ferguson/Eddie Hill
  Texas Tech-Texas A&M Ves Box/Dave Smith

- **SEPTEMBER 25, 1954**
  Oklahoma A&M-Texas A&M Dave Russell/Eddie Hill
  Texas-Notre Dame Ves Box/Jerry Doggett
  TCU-Oklahoma Kern Tips/Eddie Barker
  Baylor-Vanderbilt John Ferguson/Coit Butler
  West Texas State-Texas Tech Bob Walker/Jack Dale

- **OCTOBER 1, 1954**

  Baylor-Miami Bob Walker/Coit Butler

- **OCTOBER 2, 1954**

  Texas A&M-Georgia Ves Box/Joe Cullinane

  Washington State-Texas Dave Russell/Dave Smith

  Cornell-Rice Jerry Doggett/Jim Wiggins

  Georgia Tech-SMU Kern Tips/Mike Mistovich

  Arkansas-TCU John Ferguson/Eddie Hill

  Oklahoma A&M-Texas Tech Eddie Barker/Jack Dale

- **OCTOBER 8, 1954**

  TCU-USC Jerry Doggett/Joe Cullinane

- **OCTOBER 9, 1954**

  Rice-Wisconsin

  TCU-USC Jerry Doggett/Joe Cullinane

  Texas-Oklahoma Kern Tips/Dave Smith

  SMU-Missouri Bob Walker/Coit Butler

  Baylor-Arkansas Dave Russell/Mike Mistovich

  Texas A&M-Houston Ves Box/Eddie Hill

  Texas Western-Texas Tech Eddie Barker/Jack Dale

- **OCTOBER 16, 1954**

  TCU-Texas A&M Ves Box/Coit Butler

  Arkansas-Texas Dave Russell/Dave Smith

  Baylor-Washington John Ferguson/Eddie Barker

  SMU-Rice Kern Tips/Jerry Doggett

  Texas Tech-LSU Bob Walker/Jack Dale

- **OCTOBER 23, 1954**

  Texas-Rice Kern Tips/Bob Walker

  Texas A&M-Baylor Ves Box/Dave Smith

  Kansas-SMU Dave Russell/Coit Butler

  TCU-Penn State John Ferguson/Eddie Barker

  Texas Tech-College of the Pacific Jerry Doggett/Jack Dale

- **OCTOBER 30, 1954**
  SMU-Texas Kern Tips/Bob Walker
  Baylor-TCU Ves Box/Coit Butler
  Vanderbilt-Rice John Ferguson/Eddie Barker
  Arkansas-Texas A&M Jerry Doggett/Dave Russell

- **NOVEMBER 6, 1954**
  Texas-Baylor Ves Box/Bob Walker
  Texas A&M-SMU Dave Russell/Eddie Barker
  Rice-Arkansas Kern Tips/Jerry Doggett

- **NOVEMBER 13, 1954**
  Texas-TCU Ves Box/Eddie Barker
  Rice-Texas A&M Dave Russell/Jerry Doggett
  SMU-Arkansas Kern Tips/Bob Walker
  Tulsa-Texas Tech John Ferguson/Jack Dale

- **NOVEMBER 20, 1954**
  Baylor-SMU Kern Tips/Eddie Barker
  TCU-Rice Ves Box/Jerry Doggett
  Houston-Texas Tech John Ferguson/Jack Dale
  Arkansas-LSU Dave Russell/Bob Walker

- **NOVEMBER 25, 1954**
  Texas A&M-Texas Kern Tips/Eddie Barker

- **NOVEMBER 27, 1954**
  Rice-Baylor Kern Tips/Eddie Barker
  TCU-SMU Ves Box/Jerry Doggett
  Texas Tech-Hardin Simmons John Ferguson/Jack Dale

- **DECEMBER 4, 1954**
  Notre Dame-SMU Kern Tips/Eddie Barker

1955

- **SEPTEMBER 16, 1955**

  Texas A&M-UCLA Ves Box/Eddie Barker

- **SEPTEMBER 17, 1955**

  Texas Tech-Texas Kern Tips/Alec Chesser

  Kansas-TCU Dave Russell/Stan McKenzie

  Hardin-Simmons-Baylor Bob Walker/Dave Smith

- **SEPTEMBER 24, 1955**

  SMU-Notre Dame Dave Russell/Dave Smith

  Texas A&M-LSU Bob Walker/Eddie Hill

  Alabama-Rice Ves Box/Alec Chesser

  Tulane-Texas Stan McKenzie/Mike Mistovich

  TCU-Texas Tech Ray Cullin/Jack Dale (TV Kern Tips)

  Baylor-Villanova Eddie Barker/Coit Butler

- **OCTOBER 1, 1955**

  Texas-USC Ves Box/Coit Butler

  SMU-Georgia Tech Dave Russell/Stan McKenzie

  Texas Tech-Oklahoma A&M Ray Cullin/Jack Dale

  TCU-Arkansas Kern Tips/Jim Wiggins

  A&M-Houston Eddie Barker/Mike Mistovich

  Baylor-Maryland Jerry Doggett/Eddie Hill

  Rice-LSU Bob Walker/Alec Chesser

- **OCTOBER 7, 1955**

  Missouri-SMU Dave Russell/Alec Chesser

- **OCTOBER 8, 1955**

  Texas-Oklahoma Dave Russell/Alec Chesser (Kern Tips TV)

  Texas A&M-Nebraska Bob Walker/Coit Butler

  TCU-Alabama Stan McKenzie/Mike Mistovich

  Arkansas-Baylor Eddie Barker/Jim Wiggins

  Clemson-Rice Ves Box/Dave Smith

  Texas Tech-Texas Western Ray Cullin/Jack Dale

- **OCTOBER 15, 1955**
  Texas A&M-TCU Kern Tips/Alec Chesser
  Texas-Arkansas Ves Box/Eddie Barker
  Baylor-Washington Dave Russell/Coit Butler
  Rice-SMU Bob Walker/Dave Smith

- **OCTOBER 21, 1955**
  TCU-Miami Jerry Doggett/Stan McKenzie

- **OCTOBER 22, 1955**
  Baylor-Texas A&M Kern Tips
  Rice-Texas Ves Box/Dave Smith
  SMU-Kansas Bob Walker/Coit Butler

- **OCTOBER 29, 1955**
  Texas A&M-Arkansas Bob Walker/Jerry Doggett
  Texas-SMU Kern Tips/Alec Chesser
  Rice-Kentucky Ves Box/Coit Butler
  TCU-Baylor Dave Russell/Dave Smith

- **NOVEMBER 5, 1955**
  Arkansas-Rice Jerry Doggett/Eddie Hill
     (Kern Tips/Alec Chesser TV)
  Baylor-Texas Ves Box/Dave Smith
  SMU-Texas A&M Dave Russell/Stan McKenzie

- **NOVEMBER 12, 1955**
  Arkansas-SMU Dave Russell/Coit Butler
     (Kern Tips/Alec Chesser TV)
  Texas A&M-Rice Bob Walker/Eddie Hill
  TCU-Texas Ves Box/Dave Smith

- **NOVEMBER 19, 1955**
  Rice-TCU Ves Box/Eddie Barker
  SMU-Baylor Kern Tips/Alec Chesser

- **NOVEMBER 24, 1955**
  Texas-Texas A&M Kern Tips/Alec Chesser

- **NOVEMBER 26, 1955**

  SMU-TCU Kern Tips/Alec Chesser

  Baylor-Rice Ves Box/Eddie Barker

  Hardin-Simmons-Texas Tech Dave Russell/Ray Cullin

1956

- **SEPTEMBER 22, 1956**

  TCU-Kansas Ves Box/Jim Wiggins

  Villanova-Texas A&M John Phelan/Mike Mistovich

  Baylor-California Dave Russell/Stan McKenzie

  Alabama-Rice Eddie Barker/Carl Mann

  Notre Dame-SMU Kern Tips/Alec Chesser

  USC-Texas Bob Walker/Dave Smith

  Texas Western-Texas Tech Eddie Hill/Jack Dale

- **SEPTEMBER 29, 1956**

  Texas Tech-Baylor Eddie Barker/Jim Wiggins
      (Kern Tips Alec Chesser TV)

  Texas-Tulane Ves Box/Mike Mistovich

  Texas A&M-LSU Dave Russell/Dave Smith

  Georgia Tech-SMU Bob Walker/Eddie Hill

- **OCTOBER 6, 1956**

  Baylor-Maryland Jerry Doggett/Jim Wiggins

  SMU-Missouri Eddie Barker/Mike Mistovich

  Arkansas-TCU Kern Tips/Alec Chesser

  Texas A&M-Texas Tech Ves Box/Eddie Hill

  LSU-Rice Dave Russell/Carl Mann

  West Virginia-Texas Bob Walker/Dave Smith

- **OCTOBER 13, 1956**

  Texas A&M-Houston Eddie Barker/Carl Mann

  SMU-Duke Jerry Doggett/Mike Mistovich

  Rice-Florida Ves Box/Jim Wiggins

  TCU-Alabama Bob Walker/Stan McKenzie

  Baylor-Arkansas Dave Russell/Dave Smith

  Texas-Oklahoma TV Kern Tips/Alec Chesser

  Texas-Oklahoma Eddie Hill/Coit Butler

  West Texas State-Texas Tech John Phelan/Jack Dale

- **OCTOBER 20, 1956**

  SMU-Rice Dave Russell/Eddie Barker

  TCU-Texas A&M Ves Box/Jim Wiggins

  Arkansas-Texas Bob Walker/Dave Smith

- **OCTOBER 27, 1956**

  Texas A&M-Baylor Kern Tips/Alec Chesser

  Texas-Rice Ves Box/Jerry Doggett

  Miami-TCU Bob Walker/Eddie Barker

  Texas Tech-Arizona Dave Russell/Jim Wiggins

- **NOVEMBER 3, 1956**

  Arkansas-Texas A&M Jerry Doggett/Coit Butler
      (Kern Tips/Alec Chesser TV)

  Utah-Rice Dave Russell/Jim Wiggins

  Baylor-TCU Ves Box/Eddie Hill

  SMU-Texas Bob Walker/Dave Smith

- **NOVEMBER 10, 1956**

  TCU-Texas Tech Dave Russell/Eddie Barker

  Rice-Arkansas Ves Box/Jim Wiggins

  Texas-Baylor Bob Walker/Jerry Doggett

  Texas A&M-SMU Kern Tips/Alec Chesser

- **NOVEMBER 17, 1956**
  Texas-TCU Bob Walker/Eddie Hill
  SMU-Arkansas Dave Russell/Jim Wiggins
  Rice-Texas A&M Ves Box/Dave Smith
  Baylor-Nebraska Jerry Doggett/Mike Mistovich
  Texas Tech-Tulsa

- **NOVEMBER 24, 1956**
  TCU-Rice Ves Box
  Baylor-SMU Kern Tips

- **NOVEMBER 29, 1956**
  Texas A&M-Texas Ves Box/Eddie Barker
    (Kern Tips/Alec Chesser TV)

- **DECEMBER 1, 1956**
  Rice-Baylor Ves Box/Eddie Barker
  TCU-SMU Kern Tips/Alec Chesser
  Texas Tech-Hardin Simmons Bob Walker/Jerry Doggett

1957

- **SEPTEMBER 21, 1957**
  Maryland-Texas A&M Kern Tips/Alec Chesser
  Villanova-Baylor Eddie Hill/Dave Smith
  Rice-LSU Dave Russell/John Smith
  SMU-California Eddie Barker/Jim Wiggins
  Kansas-TCU Bob Walker/Mike Mistovich
  Texas-Georgia Ves Box/Stan McKenzie
  West Texas State-Texas Tech Jack Dale/Coit Butler

- **SEPTEMBER 28, 1957**
  SMU-Georgia Tech Eddie Barker
  TCU-Ohio State Ves Box/Jim Wiggins
  Houston-Baylor Eddie Hill/John Smith
  Tulane/Texas Dave Russell/Dave Smith
  Texas A&M-Texas Tech Bob Walker/Jack Dale

- **OCTOBER 5, 1957**
  Texas A&M-Missouri Eddie Barker/Mike Mistovich
  TCU-Arkansas Kern Tips/Alec Chesser
  Stanford-Rice
  Texas-South Carolina Ves Box/Dave Smith

- **OCTOBER 11, 1957**
  Missouri-SMU Eddie Hill/Coit Butler

- **OCTOBER 12, 1957**
  Texas-Oklahoma Jim Wiggins/Stan McKenzie
      (Kern Tips/Alec Chesser TV)
  Houston-Texas A&M Eddie Barker/Dave Smith
  Arkansas-Baylor Dave Russell/Mike Mistovich
  Duke-Rice Bob Walker/John Smith
  Alabama-TCU Ves Box/Jack Dale
  Texas Tech-Texas Western John Phelan/Rudy Tellez

- **OCTOBER 19, 1957**
  Texas-Arkansas Ves Box/Jim Wiggins
  Texas A&M-TCU Kern Tips/Alec Chesser
  Baylor-Texas Tech Bob Walker/Jack Dale
  Rice-SMU Eddie Barker/Eddie Hill

- **OCTOBER 26, 1957**
  TCU-Marquette Ves Box/Eddie Hill
  Baylor-Texas A&M Kern Tips/Alec Chesser
  Rice-Texas Bob Walker/Dave Smith
  Texas Tech-Arizona Eddie Barker/Jim Wiggins

- **NOVEMBER 2, 1957**
  Texas A&M-Arkansas Eddie Barker/Eddie Hill
  TCU-Baylor Ves Box/Dave Smith
  Texas-SMU Kern Tips/Alec Chesser
  Clemson-Rice Bob Walker/John Smith
  Texas Tech-Oklahoma State Dave Russell/Jim Wiggins

- **NOVEMBER 9, 1957**
Arkansas-Rice Bob Walker/John Smith
Baylor-Texas Ves Box/Dave Smith
Tulsa-Texas Tech Dave Russell/Jack Dale
SMU-Texas A&M Eddie Barker/Eddie Hill

- **NOVEMBER 16, 1957**
Texas A&M-Rice Ves Box/John Smith
Arkansas-SMU Kern Tips/Alec Chesser
TCU-Texas Eddie Barker/Dave Smith

- **NOVEMBER 23, 1957**
SMU-Baylor Bob Walker/Dave Smith
    (Kern Tips/Alec Chesser TV)
Rice-TCU Eddie Barker/Eddie Hill
Texas Tech-Arkansas Ves Box/John Smith

- **NOVEMBER 28, 1957**
Texas-Texas A&M Kern Tips

- **NOVEMBER 30, 1957**
Baylor-Rice Ves Box/John Smith
TCU-SMU Kern Tips/Alec Chesser

- **DECEMBER 7, 1957**
Notre Dame-SMU Kern Tips/Alec Chesser

1958

- **SEPTEMBER 20, 1958**
TCU-Kansas Dave Russell/Jack Dale
Texas A&M-Texas Tech Kern Tips/Alec Chesser
Baylor-Arkansas Bob Walker/Jim Wiggins
LSU-Rice Ves Box/John Smith
Georgia-Texas Eddie Barker/Dave Smith

- **SEPTEMBER 26, 1958**
Texas-Tulane Dave Russell/John Smith

- **SEPTEMBER 27, 1958**

  SMU-Ohio State Bob Walker/Glenn Brown
  TCU-Iowa Eddie Barker/Stan McKenzie
  Rice-Stanford Ves Box/Dave Smith
  Texas A&M-Houston Kern Tips/Alec Chesser

- **OCTOBER 4, 1958**

  Notre Dame-SMU Kern Tips/Alec Chesser
  Missouri-Texas A&M Ves Box/Stan McKenzie
  Miami-Baylor Dave Russell/Jim Wiggins
  Purdue-Rice Bob Walker/John Smith
  Arkansas-TCU Eddie Barker/Jack Dale
  Texas Tech-Texas Eddie Hill/Dave Smith

- **OCTOBER 11, 1958**

  Texas A&M-Maryland Ves Box/Stan McKenzie
  Baylor-Duke Dave Russell/Frank Glieber
  SMU-Missouri Eddie Hill/Glenn Brown
  Rice-Arkansas Bob Walker/Dave Smith
  Texas-Oklahoma Kern Tips/Alec Chesser
  Texas Tech-TCU Jim Wiggins/Jack Dale

- **OCTOBER 18, 1958**

  Baylor-Texas Tech Dave Russell/Jack Dale
      (Kern Tips/Alec Chesser TV)
  TCU-Texas A&M Eddie Barker/John Smith
  Arkansas-Texas Bob Walker/Dave Smith
  Rice-SMU Ves Box/Eddie Hill

- **OCTOBER 25, 1958**

  Georgia Tech-SMU Bob Walker/Eddie Hill
  Texas A&M-Baylor Eddie Barker/Dave Smith
  Texas-Rice Ves Box/John Smith

- **NOVEMBER 1, 1958**

  Texas Tech-Tulane Bob Walker/Jim Wiggins
  Baylor-TCU Ves Box/Eddie Hill
  SMU-Texas Kern Tips/Alec Chesser
  Arkansas-Texas A&M Eddie Barker/Dave Smith

- **NOVEMBER 8, 1958**

  Army-Rice Dave Russell/John Smith
      (Kern Tips/Alec Chesser TV)
  Texas A&M-SMU Bob Walker/Eddie Hill
  Texas-Baylor Ves Box/Dave Smith
  Arizona-Texas Tech Jim Wiggins/Jack Dale
  Marquette-TCU Eddie Barker/Stan McKenzie

- **NOVEMBER 15, 1958**

  Texas-TCU Dave Russell/Eddie Hill
      (Kern Tips/Alec Chesser TV)
  SMU-Arkansas Bob Walker/Jim Wiggins
  Texas A&M-Rice Ves Box/John Smith
  Texas Tech-Tulsa Eddie Barker/Jack Dale

- **NOVEMBER 22, 1958**

  TCU-Rice Kern Tips/Alec Chesser
  Baylor-SMU Ves Box/Eddie Hill
  Arkansas-Texas Tech Eddie Barker/Jack Dale

- **NOVEMBER 27, 1958**

  Texas A&M-Texas Kern Tips/Alec Chesser

- **NOVEMBER 29, 1958**

  Rice-Baylor Ves Box/Eddie Hill
  TCU-SMU Kern Tips/Alec Chesser
  Texas Tech-Houston Bob Walker/John Smith

1959

- **SEPTEMBER 19, 1959**

  Rice-LSU Bob Walker/Eddie Hill

  Texas-Nebraska Dave Russell/Jim Wiggins

  Texas A&M-Texas Tech Kern Tips/Alec Chesser

- **SEPTEMBER 26, 1959**

  Texas A&M-Michigan State Ves Box/Jim Wiggins

  SMU-Georgia Tech Bob Walker/Stan McKenzie

  Baylor-Colorado Dave Russell/Frank Glieber

  TCU-LSU Eddie Barker/John Smith

  Maryland-Texas Kern Tips/Alec Chesser

  Oregon State-Texas Tech Eddie Hill/Jack Dale

- **OCTOBER 3, 1959**

  California-Texas Eddie Hill/Glenn Brown

  Rice-Duke Eddie Barker/Frank Glieber

  Baylor-LSU Dave Russell/Dave Smith

  TCU-Arkansas Ves Box/Stan McKenzie

  Navy-SMU Kern Tips/Alec Chesser

  Texas A&M-Mississippi Southern Bob Walker/John Smith

  Tulsa-Texas Tech Jim Wiggins/Jack Dale

- **OCTOBER 9, 1959**

  Missouri-SMU Ves Box/Stan McKenzie

- **OCTOBER 10, 1959**

  Texas-Oklahoma Eddie Hill/Frank Glieber

    (Kern Tips/Alec Chesser TV)

  Houston-Texas A&M Bob Walker/Glenn Brown

  Arkansas-Baylor Jim Wiggins/Dave Smith

  Florida-Rice Dave Russell/John Smith

  TCU-Texas Tech Eddie Barker/Jack Dale

- **OCTOBER 17, 1959**

  Texas A&M-TCU Kern Tips/Alec Chesser
  Texas-Arkansas Bob Walker/Eddie Hill
  Texas Tech-Baylor Eddie Barker/Jim Wiggins
  SMU-Rice Ves Box/John Smith

- **OCTOBER 24, 1959**

  TCU-Pittsburgh Ves Box/John Smith
  Baylor-Texas A&M Bob Walker/Jim Wiggins
  Texas Tech-SMU Eddie Barker/Eddie Hill
  Rice-Texas Kern Tips/Alec Chesser

- **OCTOBER 31, 1959**

  Texas A&M-Arkansas Eddie Hill/Jim Wiggins
  Texas-SMU Bob Walker/Frank Glieber
  TCU-Baylor Ves Box/Dave Smith
  Clemson-Rice Eddie Barker/John Smith

- **NOVEMBER 7, 1959**

  SMU-Texas A&M Bob Walker/Dave Smith
  Baylor-Texas Kern Tips/Alec Chesser
  Arkansas-Rice Ves Box/John Smith

- **NOVEMBER 14, 1959**

  Arkansas-SMU Eddie Barker/Frank Glieber
  Texas A&M-Rice Ves Box/John Smith
  TCU-Texas Bob Walker/Dave Smith
  Houston-Texas Tech Dave Russell/Jack Dale
  Baylor-USC Eddie Hill/Jim Wiggins

- **NOVEMBER 21, 1959**

  Texas Tech-Arkansas Bob Walker/Eddie Hill
  SMU-Baylor Ves Box/Eddie Barker
  Rice-TCU Kern Tips/Alec Chesser

- **NOVEMBER 26, 1959**

  Texas-Texas A&M Kern Tips/Alec Chesser

- **NOVEMBER 28, 1959**

  Baylor-Rice Ves Box/John Smith

  SMU-TCU Kern Tips/Alec Chesser

1960

- **SEPTEMBER 17, 1960**

  SMU-Missouri Bob Walker

  TCU-Kansas Ves Box/Jim Wiggins

  Texas-Nebraska Kern Tips/Alec Chesser

  Texas A&M-LSU Eddie Barker/John Smith

- **SEPTEMBER 24, 1960**

  Texas-Maryland Ves Box/Jim Wiggins

  SMU-Ohio State Eddie Hill/Stan McKenzie

  Texas Tech-Texas A&M Eddie Barker/John Smith

  Baylor-Colorado Dave Russell/Dave Smith

  Rice-Georgia Tech Kern Tips/Alex Chesser

  TCU-LSU Bob Walker/Glenn Brown

- **OCTOBER 1, 1960**

  Texas Tech-Texas Bob Walker/Dave Smith

  Arkansas-TCU Kern Tips/Alec Chesser

  Texas A&M-Trinity Dave Russell/Jim Wiggins

  Baylor-LSU Ves Box/Eddie Hill

  Rice-Tulane Eddie Barker/John Smith

- **OCTOBER 8, 1960**

  SMU-Navy Ves Box/Glenn Brown

  Texas-Oklahoma Kern Tips/Alec Chesser

  Baylor-Arkansas Bob Walker/Jim Wiggins

  Rice-Florida Eddie Hill/Stan McKenzie

  Texas Tech-TCU Eddie Barker/Dave Smith

  Texas A&M-Houston Dave Russell/John Smith

- **OCTOBER 15, 1960**
  Arkansas-Texas Kern Tips/Alec Chesser
  Baylor-Texas Tech Eddie Barker/Jack Dale
  TCU-Texas A&M Ves Box/Jim Wiggins
  Rice-SMU Bob Walker/Eddie Hill

- **OCTOBER 22, 1960**
  Texas A&M-Baylor Eddie Barker/John Smith
  Pittsburgh-TCU Ves Box/Eddie Hill
  SMU-Texas Tech Bob Walker/Jim Wiggins
  Texas-Rice Kern Tips/Alec Chesser

- **OCTOBER 29, 1960**
  Texas Tech-Rice Bob Walker/John Smith
  Baylor-TCU Kern Tips/Alec Chesser
  SMU-Texas Ves Box/Eddie Hill
  Arkansas-Texas A&M Eddie Barker/Jim Wiggins

- **NOVEMBER 5, 1960**
  Rice-Arkansas Bob Walker
  Texas-Baylor Kern Tips/Alec Chesser
  Texas A&M-SMU Ves Box/Eddie Hill
  Tulane-Texas Tech Eddie Barker/Jack Dale

- **NOVEMBER 12, 1960**
  SMU-Arkansas Ves Box
  USC-Baylor Eddie Barker
  Texas-TCU Kern Tips
  Wyoming-Texas Tech Dave Russell

- **NOVEMBER 24, 1960**
  Texas A&M-Texas Kern Tips/Alec Chesser

- **NOVEMBER 26, 1960**
  Rice-Baylor Kern Tips
  TCU-SMU Ves Box

1961

- **SEPTEMBER 23, 1961**
  Wake Forest-Baylor Jim Wiggins/Mike Mistovich
  Texas-California Ves Box/Dave Smith
  Houston-Texas A&M Eddie Barker/John Smith
  LSU-Rice Kern Tips/Alec Chesser
  Maryland-SMU Bob Walker/Glenn Brown
  Kansas-TCU Eddie Hill/Jack Dale
  Texas Tech-Mississippi State Dave Russell/Stan McKenzie

- **SEPTEMBER 30, 1961**
  Texas Tech-Texas Kern Tips /Alec Chesser
  SMU-USC Eddie Hill/John Smith
  Baylor-Pitt Ves Box/Glenn Brown
  Rice-Georgia Tech Eddie Barker/Jim Wiggins
  TCU-Ohio State Dave Russell/Stan McKenzie
  Texas A&M-LSU Bob Walker/Dave Smith

- **OCTOBER 7, 1961**
  Air Force-SMU Eddie Barker/Eddie Hill
  TCU-Arkansas Kern Tips/Alec Chesser
  Washington State-Texas Ves Box/Jim Wiggins
  Texas A&M-Texas Tech Bob Walker/Jack Dale

- **OCTOBER 14, 1961**
  Texas-Oklahoma Kern Tips/Alec Chesser
  Texas A&M-Trinity Eddie Hill/Jim Wiggins
  Arkansas-Baylor Ves Box/Dave Smith
  Florida-Rice Bob Walker/John Smith
  TCU-Texas Tech Eddie Barker/Jack Dale

- **OCTOBER 21, 1961**
  Texas-Arkansas Kern Tips/Alec Chesser
  Texas A&M-TCU Ves Box/Eddie Hill
  SMU-Rice Eddie Barker/John Smith
  Baylor-Texas Tech Bob Walker/Stan McKenzie

- **OCTOBER 28, 1961**

  Baylor-Texas A&M Ves Box/Dave Smith

  Texas Tech-SMU Eddie Barker/Eddie Hill

  Rice-Texas Kern Tips/Alec Chesser

- **NOVEMBER 4, 1961**

  Texas A&M-Arkansas Ves Box/Jim Wiggins

  TCU-Baylor Eddie Barker/Eddie Hill

  Texas-SMU Kern Tips/Alec Chesser

  Rice-Texas Tech Bob Walker/Jack Dale

- **NOVEMBER 11, 1961**

  TCU-UCLA Eddie Hill/Jim Wiggins

  SMU-Texas A&M Eddie Barker/John Smith

  Arkansas-Rice Kern Tips/Alec Chesser

  Baylor-Texas Ves Box/Dave Smith

  Boston College-Texas Tech Bob Walker/Jack Dale

- **NOVEMBER 18, 1961`**

  Air Force-Baylor Bob Walker/Jim Wiggins

  Texas A&M-Rice Ves Box/John Smith

  Arkansas-SMU Eddie Barker/Eddie Hill

  TCU-Texas Kern Tips/Alec Chesser

- **NOVEMBER 23, 1961**

  Texas-Texas A&M Kern Tips/Alec Chesser

- **NOVEMBER 25, 1961**

  Texas Tech-Arkansas Eddie Barker/Eddie Hill

  SMU-Baylor Ves Box/Dave Smith

  Rice-TCU Kern Tips/Alec Chesser

1962

- **SEPTEMBER 22, 1962**

  Texas A&M-LSU Eddie Hill/Dave Smith

  SMU-Maryland Ves Box/Glenn Brown

  TCU-Kansas Eddie Barker/Stan McKenzie

  Baylor-Houston Jim Wiggins/John Smith

  West Texas State-Texas Tech Connie Alexander/Jack Dale

  Oregon-Texas Kern Tips/Alec Chesser

- **SEPTEMBER 29, 1962**

  USC-SMU Connie Alexander/Dave Smith

  Pitt-Baylor Jim Wiggins/John Smith

  Rice-LSU Eddie Barker/Glenn Brown

  Texas A&M-Houston Kern Tips/Alec Chesser

  TCU-Miami Eddie Hill/Stan McKenzie

  Texas-Texas Tech Ves Box/Jack Dale

- **OCTOBER 6, 1962**

  Texas Tech-Texas A&M Eddie Barker/Glenn Brown

  Air Force-SMU Eddie Hill/Stan McKenzie

  Penn State-Rice Jim Wiggins/John Smith

  Arkansas-TCU Kern Tips/Alec Chesser

  Tulane-Texas Ves Box/Dave Smith

- **OCTOBER 13, 1962**

  Baylor-Arkansas Kern Tips/Alec Chesser

  Texas-Oklahoma Eddie Hill/Glenn Brown

  Texas A&M-Florida/Stan McKenzie

  Oregon-Rice Jim Wiggins/John Smith

  Texas Tech-TCU Ves Box/Dave Smith

- **OCTOBER 20, 1962**

  TCU-Texas A&M Ves Box/Dave Smith

  Texas Tech-Baylor Eddie Hill/John Smith

  Arkansas-Texas Kern Tips/Alec Chesser

  Rice-SMU Jim Wiggins/Glenn Brown

- **OCTOBER 27, 1962**
  SMU-Texas Tech Eddie Hill/Jack Dale
  Texas A&M-Baylor Ves Box/Jim Wiggins
  Texas-Rice Kern Tips/Alec Chesser

- **NOVEMBER 3, 1962**
  Baylor-TCU Jim Wiggins/Dave Smith
  SMU-Texas Kern Tips/Alec Chesser
  Arkansas-Texas A&M Ves Box/Glenn Brown

- **NOVEMBER 10, 1962**
  Rice-Arkansas Ves Box/Dave Smith
  Texas-Baylor Kern Tips/Alec Chesser
  Texas A&M-SMU Glenn Brown/Mike Mistovich
  Texas Tech-Boston College Jim Wiggins/Stan McKenzie
  TCU-LSU Eddie Hill/John Smith

- **NOVEMBER 17, 1962**
  SMU-Arkansas Glenn Brown/Stan McKenzie
  Baylor-Air Force Jim Wiggins/Dave Smith
  Texas A&M-Rice Ves Box/John Smith
  Texas-TCU Kern Tips/Alec Chesser
  Texas Tech-Colorado Eddie Hill/Jack Dale

- **NOVEMBER 22, 1962**
  Texas A&M-Texas Kern Tips/Alec Chesser

- **NOVEMBER 24, 1962**
  TCU-Rice Kern Tips/Alec Chesser
  Arkansas-Texas Tech Eddie Hill/Jack Dale

- **DECEMBER 1, 1962**
  Rice-Baylor Ves Box/Eddie Hill
  TCU-SMU Kern Tips/Alec Chesser

1963

- **SEPTEMBER 28, 1963**

  SMU-Michigan Eddie Hill/Stan McKenzie

  Texas A&M-Ohio State Ves Box/Mike Mistovich

  Houston-Baylor Glenn Brown/John Smith

  LSU-Rice Connie Alexander/Jack Dale

  TCU-Florida State Jim Wiggins/Dave Smith

  Texas Tech-Texas Kern Tips/Alec Chesser

- **OCTOBER 5, 1963**

  TCU-Arkansas Kern Tips/Alec Chesser

  Rice-Penn State Eddie Hill/Mike Mistovich

  Air Force-SMU Jim Wiggins/John Smith

  Baylor-Oregon State Glenn Brown/Stan McKenzie

  Texas A&M-Texas Tech Ves Box/Jack Dale

  Texas-Oklahoma State Connie Alexander/Dave Smith

- **OCTOBER 12, 1963**

  Texas-Oklahoma Kern Tips/Alec Chesser

  Arkansas-Baylor Jim Wiggins/Dave Smith

  Stanford-Rice Connie Alexander/Stan McKenzie

  Houston-Texas A&M Eddie Hill/John Smith

  TCU-Texas Tech Glenn Brown/Jack Dale

- **OCTOBER 19, 1963**

  Texas-Arkansas Kern Tips/Alec Chesser

  Texas A&M-TCU Connie Alexander/Jim Wiggins

  SMU-Rice Ves Box/John Smith

  Baylor-Texas Tech Eddie Hill/Jack Dale

- **OCTOBER 26, 1963**

  Rice-Texas Kern Tips/Alec Chesser

  Texas Tech-SMU Connie Alexander/Jim Wiggins

  Baylor-Texas A&M Ves Box/Eddie Hill

- **NOVEMBER 16, 1963**
  TCU-Texas Kern Tips
  Texas A&M-Rice Connie Alexander
  Arkansas-SMU Ves Box

- **NOVEMBER 28, 1963**
  Texas-Texas A&M Kern Tips/Alec Chesser

- **NOVEMBER 30, 1963**
  Baylor-Rice Kern Tips/Alec Chesser
  SMU-TCU Ves Box/Eddie Hill

1964

- **SEPTEMBER 26, 1964**
  Baylor-Washington Jim Wiggins/Stan McKenzie
  SMU-Ohio State Ves Box/Glenn Brown
  LSU-Rice Connie Alexander/John Smith
  Florida State-TCU Eddie Hill/Jack Dale
  Texas-Texas Tech Kern Tips/Alec Chesser

- **OCTOBER 17, 1964**
  Rice-SMU
  Arkansas-Texas
  Texas Tech-Baylor
  TCU-Texas A&M

- **OCTOBER 31, 1964**
  SMU-Texas Kern Tips

- **NOVEMBER 7, 1964**
  Rice-Arkansas Connie Alexander/Glenn Brown
  Texas A&M-SMU Ves Box
  West Texas State-Texas Tech Eddie Hill

- **NOVEMBER 14, 1964**
  Washington State-Texas Tech Jack Dale
  SMU-Arkansas Kern Tips
  Texas-TCU Connie Alexander
  Texas A&M-Rice Ves Box

- **NOVEMBER 21, 1964**

  Arkansas-Texas Tech Kern Tips

- **NOVEMBER 26, 1964**

  Texas A&M-Texas Kern Tips/Alec Chesser

1965

- **SEPTEMBER 17, 1965**

  Texas-Tulane Eddie Hill/John Smith

- **SEPTEMBER 18, 1965**

  Baylor-Auburn Jack Dale/Ray Boyd
  TCU-Nebraska
  Louisiana Tech-Rice Jim Wiggins/Mike Mistovich
  SMU-Miami Ves Box/Stan McKenzie
  Texas A&M-LSU Connie Alexander/John Smith
  Kansas-Texas Tech Kern Tips/Alec Chesser

- **SEPTEMBER 25, 1965**

  Texas Tech-Texas Kern Tips/Alec Chesser
  Washington-Baylor Connie Alexander/Ray Boyd
  Florida State-TCU Glenn Brown/Stan McKenzie

- **OCTOBER 2, 1965**

  Purdue-SMU Glenn Brown/Mike Mistovich
  TCU-Arkansas Kern Tips/Alec Chesser
  Baylor-Florida State Jack Dale/Stan McKenzie
  Texas A&M-Texas Tech Eddie Hill/Ray Boyd
  Indiana-Texas Connie Alexander/Dave Smith

- **OCTOBER 9, 1965**

  Texas-Oklahoma Kern Tips/Alec Chesser
  TCU-Texas Tech Jim Wiggins/Ray Boyd
  Texas A&M-Houston Jack Dale/Dave Smith
  Arkansas-Baylor Connie Alexander/Glenn Brown

- **OCTOBER 23, 1965**
Rice-Texas Kern Tips/Alec Chesser
Texas Tech-SMU Connie Alexander/John Smith
Baylor-Texas A&M Eddie Hill
TCU-Clemson Jack Dale/Ray Boyd

- **NOVEMBER 6, 1965**
SMU-Texas A&M Connie Alexander/Dave Smith
Baylor-Texas Eddie Hill/John Smith
New Mexico State-Texas Tech Jack Dale/Ray Boyd

- **NOVEMBER 20, 1965**
Texas Tech-Arkansas Eddie Hill/John Smith
Rice-TCU Connie Alexander/Jack Dale
SMU-Baylor Kern Tips/Alec Chesser

1966

- **SEPTEMBER 17, 1966**
TCU-Nebraska Eddie Hill/Ray Boyd
Texas A&M-Georgia Tech Jim Wiggins/John Smith
Texas Tech-Kansas Kern Tips/Alec Chesser
USC-Texas Jack Dale/Stan McKenzie
Illinois-SMU Connie Alexander/Dave Smith

- **SEPTEMBER 24, 1966**
LSU-Rice Connie Alexander/John Smith/Dan Lovett
Navy-SMU Eddie Hill/Dave Smith
TCU-Ohio State
Colorado-Baylor Jim Wiggins/Ray Boyd
Texas A&M-Tulane Jack Dale/Mike Mistovich
Texas-Texas Tech Kern Tips/Alec Chesser

- **OCTOBER 1, 1966**

  Baylor-Washington State Eddie Hill/Stan McKenzie

  Rice-Tennessee Jim Wiggins/John Smith

  SMU-Purdue Glenn Brown/Ray Boyd

  Arkansas-TCU Kern Tips/Alec Chesser

  Texas Tech-Texas A&M Jack Dale/Mike Mistovich

  Indiana-Texas Connie Alexander/Dave Smith

- **OCTOBER 8, 1966**

  Baylor-Arkansas Kern Tips/Alec Chesser

  Texas Tech-TCU Connie Alexander/Ray Boyd

  UCLA-Rice Jack Dale/John Smith

  Texas-Oklahoma Eddie Hill/Dave Smith

- **OCTOBER 15, 1966**

  Arkansas-Texas Kern Tips/Alec Chesser

  TCU-Texas A&M Jack Dale/Dave Smith

  Rice-SMU Connie Alexander/Stan McKenzie

  Florida State-Texas Tech Eddie Hill/Ray Boyd

- **OCTOBER 29, 1966**

  Baylor-TCU Kern Tips/Alec Chesser

  Texas Tech-Rice Jack Dale/John Smith

  SMU-Texas Eddie Hill/Dave Smith

  Arkansas-Texas A&M Connie Alexander/Ray Boyd

- **NOVEMBER 5, 1966**

  Oklahoma State-Texas Tech Jack Dale/Ray Boyd

  Texas-Baylor Kern Tips/Alec Chesser

  Rice-Arkansas Eddie Hill/Stan McKenzie

  Texas A&M-SMU Connie Alexander/Dave Smith

- **NOVEMBER 19, 1966**

  Baylor-SMU Kern Tips/Alec Chesser

- **NOVEMBER 24, 1966**
  Texas A&M-Texas Kern Tips/Alec Chesser

- **NOVEMBER 26, 1966**
  Rice-Baylor
  SMU-TCU

- **DECEMBER 17, 1966**
  Bluebonnet Bowl
  Ole Miss-Texas Kern Tips (Tips's last game)

1967

- **SEPTEMBER 16, 1967**
  SMU-Texas A&M Eddie Hill/Dave Smith
  Baylor-Colorado Connie Alexander/Stan McKenzie

- **SEPTEMBER 23, 1967**
  Rice-LSU Connie Alexander/Ray Boyd
  SMU-Missouri Eddie Hill/Mike Mistovich
  Iowa State-Texas Tech Jack Dale/Bob Nash
  Texas-USC Ves Box/Dan Lovett
  Baylor-Syracuse Glenn Brown/Stan McKenzie
  Texas A&M-Purdue John Smith/Alec Chesser
  TCU-Iowa Jim Wiggins/Dave Smith

- **OCTOBER 7, 1967**
  TCU-Arkansas Connie Alexander/Dave Smith
  SMU-Minnesota Glenn Brown/Mike Mistovich
  Mississippi State-Texas Tech Eddie Hill/Stan McKenzie
  Florida State-Texas A&M John Smith/Alec Chesser

- **OCTOBER 13, 1967**
  Army-SMU Connie Alexander

- **OCTOBER 14, 1967**
  Texas-Oklahoma Connie Alexander

- **NOVEMBER 4, 1967**
  Texas-SMU Jack Dale/Stan McKenzie
  Texas A&M-Arkansas Connie Alexander/Dave Smith
  Rice-Texas Tech Eddie Hill/Ray Boyd

- **NOVEMBER 18, 1967**
  Texas A&M-Rice Connie Alexander
  Baylor-Texas Tech Jack Dale
  Arkansas-SMU Eddie Hill/John Smith
  TCU-Texas Glenn Brown/Dave Smith

1968

- **SEPTEMBER 21, 1968**
  Cincinnati-Texas Tech Jack Dale/Bob Nash
  Baylor/Indiana Eddie Hill/Ray Boyd
  TCU-Georgia Tech John Smith/Mike Mistovich
  SMU-Auburn Jim Wiggins
  Rice-Washington Dan Lovett
  Texas A&M-LSU Glenn Brown/Bob Hill
  Houston-Texas Connie Alexander/Dave Smith

- **SEPTEMBER 28, 1968**
  Baylor-Michigan State/Gene Arnold

- **OCTOBER 19, 1968**
  Arkansas-Texas Connie Alexander/Stan McKenzie
  Rice-SMU Dan Lovett/Dave Smith
  Texas Tech-Mississippi State
  TCU-Texas A&M

- **OCTOBER 26, 1968**
  SMU-Texas Tech Connie Alexander/Dave Smith

- **NOVEMBER 2, 1968**
  SMU-Texas Connie Alexander/Stan McKenzie
  Arkansas-Texas A&M Jack Dale/Mike Mistovich
  Baylor-TCU Dan Lovett/Bob Hill
  Texas Tech-Rice Eddie Hill/Ray Boyd

- **NOVEMBER 28, 1968**
  Texas A&M-Texas

1969

- **OCTOBER 4, 1969**
  Texas A&M-Army Jack Dale

- **OCTOBER 11, 1969**
  TCU-SMU Eddie Hill/Gene Arnold
  Texas-Oklahoma Connie Alexander/Dave Smith
  Arkansas-Baylor Jack Dale/Mike Mistovich
  Texas A&M-Texas Tech Jim Wiggins/Stan McKenzie

- **OCTOBER 18, 1969**
  Texas A&M-TCU Connie Alexander/Stan McKenzie
  SMU-Rice John Smith/Dave Smith
  Mississippi State-Texas Tech

- **NOVEMBER 8, 1969**
  SMU-Texas A&M Jack Dale/Dave Smith
  Texas Tech-TCU Eddie Hill/Ray Boyd
  Baylor-Texas Connie Alexander/Stan McKenzie
  Arkansas-Rice John Smith/Bob Hill

- **NOVEMBER 15, 1969**
  Arkansas-SMU Jack Dale/Gene Arnold
  TCU-Texas Connie Alexander/Stan McKenzie
  Baylor-Texas Tech John Smith/Bob Nash
  Texas A&M-Rice Eddie Hill/Mike Mistovich

- **NOVEMBER 22, 1969**
  SMU-Baylor Connie Alexander/Dave Smith

- **NOVEMBER 27, 1969**
  Texas-Texas A&M Connie Alexander/Dave Smith
  Texas Tech-Arkansas Eddie Hill/Stan McKenzie

- **NOVEMBER 29, 1969**
  Baylor-Rice

- **DECEMBER 6, 1969**
  Texas-Arkansas Connie Alexander/Stan McKenzie

1970

- **SEPTEMBER 19, 1970**
  Baylor-Army Connie Alexander/Stan McKenzie
  SMU-Tennessee Glenn Brown/Bob Hill
  TCU-Purdue
  Oklahoma State-Arkansas Eddie Hill/Dave Smith
  Texas A&M-LSU John Smith/Gene Arnold

- **SEPTEMBER 26, 1970**
  Texas A&M-Ohio State Dan Lovett

- **OCTOBER 10, 1970**
  Baylor-Arkansas Jack Dale/Gene Arnold
  Texas Tech-Texas A&M Eddie Hill/Stan McKenzie
  TCU-Oklahoma State
  Texas-Oklahoma

- **OCTOBER 24, 1970**
  SMU-Texas Tech Dan Lovett/Gene Arnold

- **OCTOBER 31, 1970**
  Arkansas-Texas A&M Connie Alexander/Dave Smith
  Baylor-TCU Eddie Hill/Ray Boyd
  Texas Tech-Rice John Smith/Gene Arnold
  SMU-Texas Jack Dale/Stan McKenzie

- **NOVEMBER 14, 1970**
  Texas-TCU Connie Alexander/Dave Smith

- **NOVEMBER 21, 1970**
  Arkansas-Texas Tech Connie Alexander/Stan McKenzie
  TCU-Rice Eddie Hill/Dave Smith

- **NOVEMBER 28, 1970**
  SMU-TCU Connie Alexander/Dave Smith

1971

- **SEPTEMBER 18, 1971**

  Baylor-Kansas Jim Wiggins/Mike Mistovich
  SMU-Oklahoma Eddie Hill/Ray Boyd
  Texas-UCLA Connie Alexander/Stan McKenzie
  UTA-TCU Frank Fallon/Bob Hill
  New Mexico-Texas Tech Jack Dale/Bob Nash
  USC-Rice Glenn Brown/Gene Arnold
  Texas A&M-LSU

- **OCTOBER 16, 1971**

  Texas-Arkansas Connie Alexander/Dave Smith
  Texas A&M-TCU Jack Dale/Stan McKenzie
  SMU-Rice Eddie Hill/Ron Stone
  Boston College-Texas Tech Glenn Brown/Bob Nash

- **OCTOBER 23, 1971**

  Rice-Texas Connie Alexander/Stan McKenzie
  Baylor-Texas A&M John Smith/Gene Arnold
  TCU-Penn State Glenn Brown/Mike Mistovich
  Texas Tech-SMU Jack Dale/Dave Smith

- **OCTOBER 30, 1971**

  Rice-Texas Tech Jack Dale/Ray Boyd
  Texas-SMU Eddie Hill/Stan McKenzie
  Texas A&M-Arkansas Connie Alexander/Dave Smith
  TCU-Baylor Jim Wiggins/Gene Arnold

- **NOVEMBER 6, 1971**

  Texas Tech-TCU Eddie Hill/Dave Smith
  SMU-Texas A&M Jack Dale/Gene Arnold
  Baylor-Texas
  Arkansas-Rice

- **NOVEMBER 13, 1971**
  Baylor-Texas Tech Glenn Brown/Ray Boyd
  TCU-Texas Connie Alexander/Stan McKenzie
  Texas A&M-Rice
  Arkansas-SMU Eddie Hill/Dave Smith

- **NOVEMBER 25, 1971**
  Texas-Texas A&M Connie Alexander/Dave Smith

- **NOVEMBER 27, 1971**
  TCU-SMU Connie Alexander/Stan McKenzie
  Baylor-Rice John Smith/Gene Arnold

1972

- **SEPTEMBER 9, 1972**
  Texas A&M-Wichita State John Smith/Gene Arnold
  Houston-Rice Connie Alexander/Dave Smith

- **SEPTEMBER 23, 1972**
  Baylor-Missouri Frank Fallon/Mike Mistovich
  Clemson-Rice Eddie Hill/Gene Arnold
  SMU-Florida John Smith/Ron Stone
  Miami-Texas Jack Dale/Stan McKenzie
  Texas A&M-LSU Connie Alexander/Dave Smith
  TCU-Indiana Jim Wiggins/Bob Hill
  Texas Tech-New Mexico Glenn Brown/Ray Boyd

- **SEPTEMBER 30, 1972**
  SMU-Virginia Tech Eddie Hill/Ray Boyd
  Rice-Georgia Tech John Smith/Gene Arnold
  Texas-Texas Tech Connie Alexander/Stan McKenzie
  Army-A&M Glenn Brown/Mike Mistovich
  UTA-TCU Frank Fallon/Bob Hill

- **OCTOBER 14, 1972**
  Baylor-Arkansas Jack Dale/Dave Smith
  Texas-Oklahoma Connie Alexander/Stan McKenzie
  Texas Tech-Texas A&M John Smith/Ray Boyd
  TCU-Tulsa Jim Wiggins/Bob Hill

- **OCTOBER 21, 1972**
  TCU-Texas A&M Jack Dale/Stan McKenzie
  Rice-SMU
  Arkansas-Texas Connie Alexander/Dave Smith
  Arizona-Texas Tech Jim Wiggins/Mike Mistovich

- **OCTOBER 28, 1972**
  Texas A&M-Baylor Glenn Brown/Dave Smith
  Texas-Rice Connie Alexander/Stan McKenzie
  Texas Tech-SMU John Smith/Ray Boyd
  TCU-Notre Dame Jack Dale/Bob Hill

- **NOVEMBER 4, 1972**
  Arkansas-Texas A&M Connie Alexander/Dave Smith
  Baylor-TCU Eddie Hill/Ron Stone
  Rice-Texas Tech John Smith/Gene Arnold
  SMU-Texas Frank Fallon/Stan McKenzie

- **NOVEMBER 25, 1972**
  Arkansas-Texas Tech Connie Alexander/Stan McKenzie
  TCU-Rice John Smith/Ron Stone
  Baylor-SMU Jack Dale/Gene Arnold

1973

- **SEPTEMBER 15, 1973**
  Oklahoma-Baylor Connie Alexander/Dave Smith
  Rice-Houston Jack Dale/John Smith
  Santa Clara-SMU Eddie Hill/Stan McKenzie
  Wichita State-Texas A&M Frank Fallon/Gene Arnold
  Utah-Texas Tech Jim Wiggins/Ray Boyd

- **SEPTEMBER 22, 1973**
  Texas-Miami Eddie Hill/Dave Smith
  Texas A&M-LSU Connie Alexander/Stan McKenzie
  SMU-Oregon State Jack Dale/Gene Arnold
  Texas Tech-New Mexico Glenn Brown/Ray Boyd
  UTA-TCU /Tim Osborne
  Baylor-Pitt Frank Fallon/Ron Stone

- **SEPTEMBER 29, 1973**
  Baylor-Colorado Jack Dale/John Smith
  Rice-LSU Frank Fallon/Gene Arnold
  SMU-Virginia Tech Glenn Brown/Ray Boyd
  Texas Tech-Texas Connie Alexander/Dave Smith
  Texas A&M-Boston College Tom Hedrick/Ron Stone
  TCU-Ohio State Eddie Hill/Stan McKenzie

- **OCTOBER 6, 1973**
  Texas A&M-Clemson Jim Wiggins/Gene Arnold
  Missouri-SMU Frank Fallon/Dave Smith
  Florida State-Baylor Glenn Brown/Ray Boyd
  Texas Tech-Oklahoma State Eddie Hill/Ron Stone
  Wake Forest-Texas Jack Dale/Stan McKenzie
  TCU-Arkansas Connie Alexander/John Smith

- **OCTOBER 13, 1973**
  Texas-Oklahoma Connie Alexander/Stan McKenzie
  Arkansas-Baylor Eddie Hill/Dave Smith
  Texas A&M-Texas Tech Frank Fallon/Ron Stone
  Notre Dame-Rice Jack Dale/John Smith
  Idaho-TCU

- **OCTOBER 20, 1973**
  Texas-Arkansas Connie Alexander/Dave Smith
  SMU-Rice Jack Dale/Gene Arnold
  TCU-Texas A&M Glenn Brown/John Smith
  Texas Tech-Arizona Jim Wiggins/Stan McKenzie

- **OCTOBER 27, 1973**

  Baylor-Texas A&M Jack Dale/Dave Smith
  SMU-Texas Tech Connie Alexander/Stan McKenzie
  Rice-Texas Frank Fallon/John Smith
  TCU-Tennessee Eddie Hill/Ray Boyd

- **NOVEMBER 3, 1973**

  Rice-Texas Tech Eddie Hill/John Smith
  TCU-Baylor Jim Wiggins/Ron Stone
  Texas A&M-Arkansas Glenn Brown/Gene Arnold
  Texas-SMU Connie Alexander/Dave Smith

- **NOVEMBER 10, 1973**

  Arkansas-Rice Frank Fallon/Ron Stone
  Baylor-Texas Connie Alexander/John Smith
  SMU-Texas A&M Jack Dale/Stan McKenzie
  Texas Tech-TCU Eddie Hill/Dave Smith

1974

- **SEPTEMBER 14, 1974**

  Baylor-Oklahoma Jack Dale/John Smith
  North Texas-SMU Tom Hedrick/Tim Osborne
  Texas-Boston College Connie Alexander/Stan McKenzie
  Clemson-Texas A&M Frank Fallon/Dave Smith
  UTA-TCU Eddie Hill/Bob Barry
  Iowa State-Texas Tech Jim Wiggins/Ray Boyd
  Houston-Rice Glenn Brown/Gene Arnold

- **SEPTEMBER 21, 1974**

  Baylor-Missouri Tom Hedrick/Stan McKenzie
  SMU-Virginia Tech Frank Fallon/Bob Barry
  Texas-Wyoming Glenn Brown/John Smith
  Texas A&M-LSU Connie Alexander/Dave Smith
  TCU-Arizona State Jim Wiggins/Ray Boyd
  Texas Tech-New Mexico Jack Dale/Gene Arnold
  Rice-Cincinnati Eddie Hill/Tim Osborne

- **SEPTEMBER 28, 1974**
  Oklahoma State-Baylor Frank Fallon-Tim Osborne
  SMU-Ohio State Eddie Hill/Dave Smith
  Texas-Texas Tech Connie Alexander/Stan McKenzie
  LSU-Rice Tom Hedrick/John Smith
  TCU-Minnesota Glenn Brown/Ray Boyd
  Texas A&M-Washington Jack Dale/Gene Arnold

- **OCTOBER 5, 1974**
  Arkansas-TCU Connie Alexander/John Smith
  Texas A&M-Kansas Eddie Hill/Stan McKenzie
  Washington-Texas Frank Fallon/Dave Smith
  Oklahoma State-Texas Tech Jack Dale/Ray Boyd
  Baylor-Florida State Jim Wiggins/Gene Arnold
  Oregon State-SMU Tom Hedrick/Bob Barry

- **OCTOBER 12, 1974**
  Texas Tech-Texas A&M Jack Dale/John Smith
  Rice-Notre Dame Frank Fallon/Gene Arnold
  Baylor-Arkansas Glenn Brown/Ray Boyd
  SMU-TCU Eddie Hill/Stan McKenzie
  Texas-Oklahoma Connie Alexander/Dave Smith

- **OCTOBER 19, 1974**
  Arkansas-Texas Connie Alexander/Stan McKenzie
  TCU-Texas A&M Jack Dale/Dave Smith
  Rice-SMU Tom Hedrick/John Smith
  Arizona-Texas Tech Eddie Hill/Ray Boyd

- **OCTOBER 26, 1974**
  TCU-Alabama Frank Fallon/Gene Arnold
  Texas Tech-SMU Jim Wiggins/Stan McKenzie

- **NOVEMBER 2, 1974**
  Arkansas-Texas A&M Connie Alexander/Ray Boyd
  SMU-Texas Jack Dale/John Smith
  Baylor-TCU Eddie Hill/Gene Arnold
  Texas Tech-Rice Glenn Brown/Tim Osborne

- **NOVEMBER 9, 1974**

  Rice-Arkansas Eddie Hill/Dave Smith
  Texas A&M-SMU Frank Fallon/John Smith
  TCU-Texas Tech Jack Dale/Ray Boyd
  Texas-Baylor Connie Alexander/Stan McKenzie

- **NOVEMBER 16, 1974**

  SMU-Arkansas Glenn Brown/Gene Arnold
  Rice-Texas A&M Connie Alexander/Dave Smith
  Texas-TCU Eddie Hill/Stan McKenzie
  Texas Tech-Baylor Jim Wiggins/John Smith

- **NOVEMBER 23, 1974**

  Baylor-SMU Connie Alexander/Stan McKenzie
  Arkansas-Texas Tech Jack Dale/Ray Boyd
  TCU-Rice Eddie Hill/John Smith

- **NOVEMBER 29, 1974**

  Texas A&M-Texas Connie Alexander/Dave Smith

- **NOVEMBER 30, 1974**

  Rice-Baylor Connie Alexander/John Smith

1975

- **SEPTEMBER 13, 1975**

  Rice-Houston Frank Fallon/John Smith
  SMU-Florida Eddie Hill/Gene Arnold
  Colorado State-Texas Glenn Brown/Dave Smith
  Mississippi State-Texas A&M Connie Alexander/Stan McKenzie
  Florida State-Texas Tech Jack Dale/Ray Boyd

- **SEPTEMBER 20, 1975**

  Auburn-Baylor Jim Wiggins/Dave Smith
  Texas-Washington Jack Dale/Gene Arnold
  Texas A&M-LSU Connie Alexander/Stan McKenzie
  Arizona State-TCU Frank Fallon/Bob Barry
  New Mexico-Texas Tech Glenn Brown/Ray Boyd
  Vanderbilt-Rice Eddie Hill/John Smith

- **OCTOBER 4, 1975**
  Texas A&M-Kansas State Eddie Hill/Dave Smith
  Utah State-Texas Glenn Brown/Stan McKenzie
  TCU-Arkansas Connie Alexander/John Smith

- **OCTOBER 11, 1975**
  Texas-Oklahoma Connie Alexander/Stan McKenzie
  Arkansas-Baylor Frank Fallon/John Smith
  Texas A&M-Texas Tech Jack Dale/Dave Smith
  Mississippi State-Rice Glenn Brown/Gene Arnold

- **OCTOBER 18, 1975**
  Texas A&M-TCU Jack Dale/Stan McKenzie
  Texas-Arkansas Connie Alexander/Dave Smith
  SMU-Rice Eddie Hill/John Smith
  Texas Tech-Arizona

- **NOVEMBER 1, 1975**
  Texas-SMU Connie Alexander/Stan McKenzie
  Rice-Texas Tech Jack Dale/Gene Arnold
  TCU-Baylor Jim Wiggins/John Smith

- **NOVEMBER 8, 1975**
  SMU-Texas A&M Frank Fallon/Dave Smith
  Arkansas-Rice Stan McKenzie
  Baylor-Texas Connie Alexander/John Smith
  Texas Tech-TCU Eddie Hill/Ray Boyd

- **NOVEMBER 15, 1975**
  TCU-Texas Glenn Brown/Dave Smith
  Texas A&M-Rice Connie Alexander/John Smith
  Baylor-Texas Tech Jack Dale/Gene Arnold
  Arkansas-SMU Eddie Hill/Stan McKenzie

- **NOVEMBER 22, 1975**
  Texas Tech-Arkansas Connie Alexander/Stan McKenzie
  SMU-Baylor Jack Dale/John Smith
  Rice-TCU Frank Fallon/Dave Smith

1976

- **SEPTEMBER 11, 1976**

  Utah State-Arkansas Jim Wiggins/Gene Arnold
  Colorado-Texas Tech
  Houston-Baylor Connie Alexander/Dave Smith
  Texas-Boston College Glenn Brown/Stan McKenzie
  Virginia Tech-Texas A&M Frank Fallon/Dave South
  TCU-SMU

- **SEPTEMBER 25, 1976**

  Tulsa-Arkansas Glenn Brown/Ray Boyd
  Texas A&M-Houston Connie Alexander/Gene Arnold

- **OCTOBER 16, 1976**

  Houston-SMU Eddie Hill/John Smith
  Texas Tech-Rice Jack Dale/Gene Arnold
  Baylor-Texas A&M Connie Alexander/Stan McKenzie

- **OCTOBER 23, 1976**

  Arkansas-Houston Connie Alexander/John Smith/Gene Arnold
  Rice-Texas A&M Jack Dale/Stan McKenzie
  SMU-Texas Gene Elston/Bob Barry
  Arizona-Texas Tech Frank Fallon/Ray Boyd
  TCU-Miami Eddie Hill/Dave South

- **OCTOBER 30, 1976**

  Texas-Texas Tech Connie Alexander/Stan McKenzie/Jack Dale
  TCU-Houston Gene Elston/Dave South
  Rice-Arkansas Glenn Brown/Bob Barry
  Texas A&M-SMU Frank Fallon/John Smith

- **NOVEMBER 13, 1976**

  Texas A&M-Arkansas Connie Alexander/Stan McKenzie
  Baylor-Rice Gene Elston/John Smith
  SMU-Texas Tech Jack Dale/Ray Boyd
  Texas-TCU Glenn Brown/Dave South

1977

- **SEPTEMBER 10, 1977**

  Kansas-Texas A&M Frank Fallon/Ray Boyd
  Boston College-Texas Glenn Brown/Dave South
  SMU-TCU

- **SEPTEMBER 17, 1977**

  Kentucky-Baylor John Smith/Dave South
  Houston-Penn State Connie Alexander/Stan McKenzie
  Florida-Rice Eddie Hill/Ron Stone
  New Mexico-Texas Tech Jim Wiggins/Ray Boyd
  North Texas-SMU Gene Elston/Bob Dahlgren
  Virginia-Texas Frank Fallon/Mike Edmonds
  Texas A&M-Virginia Tech Jack Dale/Bob Barry
  Oregon-TCU Glenn Brown/Hal Chesnut

- **SEPTEMBER 24, 1977**

  Texas A&M-Texas Tech Connie Alexander/Ray Boyd

- **OCTOBER 1, 1977**

  Texas A&M-Michigan Connie Alexander

- **OCTOBER 8, 1977**

  Texas-Oklahoma Connie Alexander

- **OCTOBER 15, 1977**

  Texas-Arkansas Connie Alexander/Stan McKenzie
  Rice-Texas Tech Glenn Brown/Dave South
  SMU-Houston Frank Fallon/Gene Arnold
  Texas A&M-Baylor Jack Dale/Dave Smith

- **OCTOBER 22, 1977**

  Air Force-Baylor Jim Wiggins/Dave South
  Texas-SMU Jack Dale/John Smith
  Miami-TCU Eddie Hill/Stan McKenzie
  Texas A&M-Rice Gene Elston/Gene Arnold
  Houston-Arkansas Connie Alexander/Ray Boyd

- **OCTOBER 29, 1977**
Arkansas-Rice Jack Dale/Gene Arnold
Houston-TCU Gene Elston/John Smith
SMU-Texas A&M Frank Fallon/Stan McKenzie
Texas Tech-Texas Connie Alexander/Dave Smith

- **NOVEMBER 5, 1977**
Baylor-Arkansas Connie Alexander/Dave Smith
Texas-Houston Frank Fallon/Stan McKenzie
Rice-SMU Glenn Brown/John Smith
TCU-Texas Tech Jack Dale/Ray Boyd

- **NOVEMBER 12, 1977**
Arkansas-Texas A&M Connie Alexander/Stan McKenzie
Rice-Baylor Gene Elston/Dave South
Texas Tech-SMU Frank Fallon/Dave Smith
TCU-Texas Jack Dale/John Smith

- **NOVEMBER 19, 1977**
SMU-Arkansas Glenn Brown/Gene Arnold
Baylor-Texas Connie Alexander/Dave Smith
Texas Tech-Houston Frank Fallon/Stan McKenzie
Texas A&M-TCU Jack Dale/John Smith

- **NOVEMBER 26, 1977**
TCU-Baylor Frank Fallon/Dave South
Houston-Rice Jack Dale/Dave Smith
Texas-Texas A&M Connie Alexander/Stan McKenzie/Glenn Brown

- **DECEMBER 3, 1977**
Houston-Texas A&M Connie Alexander/Dave Smith

APPENDIX 7

Kern Tips Memorial Award Recipients

From 1968-1976, the Kern Tips Memorial Award was presented to a senior football player in the Southwest Conference. Each school nominated a player with high academic standing, high morals, sportsmanship, and athletic ability. A panel of SWC officials, University officials, sportswriters, and Humble announcers selected the winner.

1968	Chris Gilbert	Texas
1969	Buster Adami	Texas A&M
1970	Bill Burnett	Arkansas
1971	Gary Hammond	SMU
1972	Robert Popelka	SMU
1973	Joe Barnes	Texas Tech
1974	Neal Jeffrey	Baylor
1975	Marty Akins	Texas
1976	Brian Hall	Texas Tech

BIBLIOGRAPHY-SOURCES

BOOKS

Barker, Eddie and John Mark Dempsey. *Eddie Barker's Notebook,* John M. Hardy Publishing Company, 2006.

Dent, Jim. *The Junction Boys—How Ten Days in Hell with Bear Bryant Forged a Championship Team,* St. Martin's Griffin, 2000.

Evans, Wilbur (ed.). *The Official Southwest Athletic Conference Football Roster and Record Book,* The Southwest Athletic Conference, 1967, Volume XVIII.

Gregory, Lloyd J. *Looking 'Em Over, Tales of a Texas Sports Writer,* Steck-Warlick Company, 1968.

Harris, Jack, Jack McGrew, and Paul Huhndorff. *The Fault Does Not Lie with Your Set: The First Forty Years of Houston Television,* Eakin Press, 1989.

Hedrick, Tom. *The Art of Sportscasting: How to Build a Successful Career,* Taylor Trade Publishing, 2012.

Holley, Joe. *Slingin' Sam: The Life and Times of the Greatest Quarterback Ever to Play the Game,* University of Texas Press, 2012.

Jenkins, Dan. *Fast Copy,* Simon & Schuster, 1988.

Larson, Henrietta M. and Kevin Wiggins Porter. *History of Humble Oil & Refining Company; A Study in Industrial Growth,* Harper, 1959.

Lovett, Daniel J. *Anybody Seen Dan Lovett? Memoirs of a Media Nomad,* Balboa Press, 2014.

Lundquist, Verne. *Play by Play: Calling the Wildest Games in Sports, from SEC Football to College Basketball, The Masters, and More,* HarperCollins Publishers, 2018.

MacCambridge, Michael. *Lamar Hunt: A Life in Sports,* Andrews McMeel Publishing LLC, Kansas City, 2012.

McLendon, Gordon. *The Maverick of Radio,* Praeger, 1992.

Mercer, Bill. *Play-by-Play Tales by a Sports Broadcasting Insider,* Taylor Trade Publishing, 2007.

Oriard, Michael. *King Football: Sport and Spectacle in the Golden Age of Radio and Newsreels, Movies and Magazines, the Weekly and the Daily Press,* The University of North Carolina Press, 2004.

Nelson, Lindsey. *Hello Everybody, I'm Lindsey Nelson,* Beech Tree Books, 1985.

Patterson, Ted. *The Golden Voices of Football,* Sports Publishing LLC, 2004.

Payne, Charles F, with Dick Hitt. *Feedback—Echoes from My Life in Radio,* Ruby Moon, 2000.

Pilkington, Tom. *State of Mind—Texas Literature and Culture,* Texas A&M University Press, 1998.

Purvis, Hoyt and Stanley Sharp (contributor). *Voices of the Razorbacks: A History of Arkansas's Iconic Sports Broadcasters,* Butler Center for Arkansas Studies, 2013.

Ratliff, Harold V. *The Power and the Glory—The Story of Southwest Conference Football,* The Texas Tech Press, 1957.

Russell Jan Jarboe. *Lady Bird: A Biography of Mrs. Johnson,* Scribner, 1999.

Schroeder, Richard. *Texas Signs On: The Early Days of Radio and Television*, Centennial Series of the Association of Former Students, Texas A&M University, Texas A&M Press, 1998

Shropshire, Mike. *Johnny Football, Johnny Manziel's Wild Ride from Obscurity to Legend at Texas A&M*, MVP Books, 2014.

Shropshire, Mike. *Runnin' with the Big Dogs: The Long, Twisted History of the Texas-OU Rivalry*, William Morrow, 2006.

Smith, Ronald A. *Play-by-Play: Radio, Television, and Big-Time College Sport*, Johns Hopkins University Press, 2001.

Southwest Conference media relations staff. *Southwest Conference Records Book*, 1914-1996.

Sterling, Ross S., and Ed Kilman and Don Carleton (ed.), *Ross Sterling, Texan: A Memoir by the Founder of Humble Oil and Refining Company*, University of Texas Press, 2012.

Stockdale, Ken. *Southwest Conference football: The classic 60's*, Companion Press, 1992.

St. John, Bob. *Texas Sports Writers: The Wild and Wacky Years*, Taylor Trade Publishing, 2001.

Tips, Kern. *Football Texas Style: An Illustrated History of the Southwest Conference*, Doubleday & Company, 1964.

Woolley, Lynn. *The Last Great Days of Radio*, Republic of Texas Press, 1994.

MAGAZINE ARTICLES

Cartwright, Gary. "0:00 to Go Time Has Run out on the Southwest Conference, but What a Time It Was," *Sports Illustrated*, October 30, 1995.

Halberstam, David J. "Verne Lundquist; a Hearty Laugh and Natural Warmth that Might Never be Replaced," *Sports Business Journal*, May 20, 2018.

NEWSPAPER ARTICLES

Associated Press, "Connie Alexander—Announcer Puts Heart into Work," *Denton Record Chronicle*, November 19, 1970.

Barron, David, "It's Last Call for A&M Broadcaster Dave South," *Houston Chronicle*, December 28, 2017.

Burton, Alan, "Glory Days of SWC Recalled by Humble Memories," *Sherman Democrat*, September 12, 1995.

Chapa, Chino, "Changes May Be Drastic for SWC Network," *The University Daily*, Texas Tech University, March 1, 1978.

Chapa, Chino, "Network Adds Bid for SWC Coverage," *The University Daily*, January 27, 1978.

Chapa, Chino, "TSN to Drop Suit Against SWC for Football Rights," *The University Daily*, February 22, 1978.

Chapa, Chino, "New Formulas No Relief for Stations," *The University Daily*, March 2, 1978.

Chapa, Chino, "Officials to Discuss SWC Coverage," *The University Daily*, December 4, 1978.

Chapo, Chino, "Mutual May Have Violated Contract," *The University Daily*, December 4, 1978.

Chapo, Chino, "Small Markets Pleased with Mutual," *The University Daily*, December 7, 1978.

El Paso Times, "Casper Remains Addicted to Radio," April 14, 1985.

Ferguson, Jim, "Testing, One, Two, Three," *Lubbock Avalanche-Journal*, 1979.

Gallagher, Jack, "SWC Turns Off Exxon," *Houston Post*, circa 1978.

The Malakoff News, "History of Humble Football Broadcasts," September 12, 1958.

Pettit, Burle, "The Contrasting Worlds of Jack Dale," *Lubbock Avalanche-Journal*, February 20, 1969.

Pettit, Burle, "Dale Was Holdover from Golden Era of Sportscasters," *Lubbock Avalanche-Journal*, August 5, 2011.

Pettit, Burle, "SWC Is but a Memory of Simpler Times of Yore," *Lubbock Avalanche-Journal*, December 19, 2015.

Smith, Toby, "Alexander Wants Back In," *Albuquerque Journal*, October 7, 2008.

Smith, Tumbleweed, "Tumbleweed Tales," *Odessa American*, November 25, 1990.

Smith, Tumbleweed, "A Tribute to Kern Tips," *The Eldorado Success*, September 4, 1997.

Tagliabue, Emil, "The Men Behind the Voices in SWC Radio Booths," *Corpus Christi Caller-Times*, November 26, 1975.

United Press, "Mutual Receives SWC Broadcasting Rights," *The Port Arthur News*, May 7, 1978.

NEWSPAPERS

Abilene Reporter News
Albany News
Albuquerque Journal
Alto Herald
Amarillo News Globe
Andrews County News
Austin American-Statesman
Ballinger Ledger
Baird Star
Bay City News
Baytown Sun
Bellville Times
Belton Journal
Big Lake Wildcat
Big Spring Daily Herald
Brackett News-Mail
Brookshire Times
Brownsville Herald
Brownwood Bulletin
Bryan Eagle
Burleson County Ledger
Caldwell News
Cameron Herald
Cisco News
Cisco Press
Clifton Record
Coleman Democrat-Voice
Corpus Christi Caller Times
Cross Plains Review
Daily Texan (University of Texas)
Dallas Morning News
Del Rio News Herald
Denison Herald
Denison Press
Denton Record Chronicle

Eastland Telegram
Edna Herald
Eldorado Success
El Paso Times
Ennis Daily News
Fayetteville Arkansas Northwest Times
Fort Worth Star-Telegram
Fredericksburg Standard
Friona Star
Gatesville Messenger & Star-Forum
Gilmer Mirror
Goldthwaite Eagle
Gorman Progress
Greenville Evening Banner
Harlingen Valley Morning Star
Haskell Free Press
Herald Democrat
Hondo Anvil Herald
Houston Chronicle
Houston Post
Humble Football News
Iowa Park Herald
Irving News Record
Jacksboro Gazette-News
Kerrville Mountain Sun
Knox County Herald
Lockhart Post-Register
Longview News-Journal
Lubbock Avalanche-Journal
Malakoff News
Marion County Courier
McAllen Monitor
McLean News
Menard News

Memphis Democrat
Mercedes Enterprise
Mineola Monitor
Muenster Enterprise
Olney Enterprise
Orange Leader
Ozona Stockman
Palacios Beacon
Pampa Daily News
Port Arthur News
Post Dispatch
Putnam News
Rising Star Record
Robstown Record
Rockdale Reporter
Ropes Plainsman
Rusk Cherokeean
Saint Jo Tribune
San Antonio Express-News
San Antonio Light
San Benito News
San Patricio County News
San Saba News and Star
Santa Anna News
Sealy News
Seminole Sentinel
Sherman Democrat
Shiner Gazette
Silsbee Bee
Slaton Slatonite
Stephens County Sun
Sweetwater Reporter
Timpson Weekly Times
Taft Tribune
Taylor Daily Press
Toreador (Texas Tech)

Waco News-Citizen
Waco Tribune-Herald
Waxahachie Daily Light
Weimer Mercury
Whitewright Sun
Wichita Falls Record News
The University Daily (Texas Tech)
Vernon Times
Victoria Advocate
Yoakum County Review
Yoakum Herald-Times

POEM
Starry, Ron, "A Tribute to Kern Tips."

REPORTS, OTHER
Jones, W. Dwayne, 1016 Update by Shonda Mace and David W. Moore, Jr., A Field Guide to Gas Stations in Texas, Historical Studies Report No. 2003-03, Texas Department of Transportation, Environmental Affairs Division, Historical Studies Branch

Oxley, Billy B., "A Descriptive Analysis of the Radio Sportscasting Techniques of Kern Tips," Master's thesis, University of Texas, 1965.

AUTHOR INTERVIEWS

Jack Dale   phone 9-11-95
Steve Fallon   phone 2-7-19
Mike Fallon   phone 2-7-19
Tom Hedrick   phone 3-7-19
Dan Lovett   phone 3-6-19
John Morris   phone 3-8-19

OTHER INTERVIEWS, SOURCES

Connie Alexander oral interview, University of New Mexico, University Libraries Center for Southwest Research and Special Collections

James Hulsman, Albuquerque High School Sports History Collection, Box 1, Folder 27, Center for Southwest Research, University Libraries, University of New Mexico

Rural Radio Magazine

RADIO/AUDIO/TRANSCRIBED TAPES

Alexander, Connie Oral History Interview, December 8, 2015. Interview by William Tydeman, Online Transcription, Southwest Collection/Special Collections Library, Texas Tech University, accessed February 7, 2019.

McGuff, Mike, KWBU, radio interview with Frank Fallon and John Morris, February 1999.

Patterson, Ted. *The Golden Voices of Football*, CD includes 69 tracks of game calls, reactions, and interviews, 2004.

Prince-Jones, Jane. KFYO radio interview with Jack Dale, April 23, 2002.

PLAY-BY-PLAY BROADCAST AUDIO TAPES

1969 Texas vs. Arkansas, Connie Alexander, Stan McKenzie, Humble Radio Network

1970 Cotton Bowl, Texas vs. Notre Dame, Connie Alexander, Jack Buck, CBS Radio

1971 Cotton Bowl, Texas vs. Notre Dame, Connie Alexander, Tom Hedrick, CBS Radio

1974 Cotton Bowl, Nebraska vs. Texas, Connie Alexander, Tom Hedrick, CBS Radio

1977 Cotton Bowl, Maryland vs. Houston, Connie Alexander, Tom Hedrick, CBS Radio

1977 TCU vs. Texas, Jack Dale, John Smith, Exxon Radio Network

1978 Cotton Bowl, Notre Dame vs. Texas, Connie Alexander, Tom Hedrick, CBS Radio

WEBSITES

Carleton, Don. "Cronkite's Texas: A Q & A with Walter Cronkite," news.utexas.edu, December 4, 2009.

Einerwold, Chelsea. "Lobo Baseball Alumni: Connie Alexander," *golobos.com*, November 15, 2011.

http://susannataliefreeman.com/SWCfootball.html

Simon, Matt. "Spotlight: "Thankful," 12thman.com, November 9, 2017.

http://swco.ttu.edu/Reference/Collections/NewspaperLists/newspaper.php
(Texas Tech Southwest Collection Special Collections Library).

"UNM, Texas Tech Receive Sports Broadcast Collections from Connie Alexander," The University of New Mexico Newsroom, January 27, 2016.

https://tshaonline.org/handbookThe Handbook of Texas Online

www.hornfans.com, 2007

www.texashistory.unt.edu

ABOUT THE AUTHOR

Throughout a professional writing career spanning nearly forty years, Alan Burton has received awards from the Associated Press, Texas School Public Relations Association, and Oklahoma College Public Relations Association.

The Sherman, Texas, native is the author of seven books.

Burton has thirty-seven years of experience in the media/communications field and currently serves as special assistant to the president and director of university communications at Southeastern Oklahoma State University. He has been associated with the Durant, Oklahoma, university for nineteen years in various capacities. He was director of community relations for eleven years for the Sherman Independent School District and a former sports editor at the *Sherman Democrat*.

Burton is a 1979 graduate of Texas Tech University, where he earned a bachelor of arts degree in English.

OTHER BOOKS BY ALAN BURTON

Til the Fat Lady Sings . . . Classic Texas Sports Quotes,
Texas Tech University Press, 1994.

Rave On . . . Classic Texas Music Quotes,
Texas Tech University Press, 1996.

Texas High School Hotshots . . . The Stars Before They Were Stars,
Republic of Texas Press, 2002.

Dallas Cowboys Quips and Quotes,
State House Press, 2006.

Pirates, Soldiers & Fat Little Girlfriends . . . More Classic Texas Sports Quotes,
Zone Press, 2010.

*Squib-Kick It to a Fat Guy . . . and 699 More Memorable Quotes
from the Playbook of Coach Mike Leach,*
Anarene Books, 2016.

www.ingramcontent.com/pod-product-compliance
Lightning Source LLC
Chambersburg PA
CBHW022142050726

47590CB00002B/550